# THE SUCCESS SYNDROME

## Hitting Bottom
## When You Reach The Top

# THE SUCCESS SYNDROME

## Hitting Bottom
## When You Reach The Top

## Dr. Steven Berglas

PLENUM PRESS • NEW YORK AND LONDON

Library of Congress Cataloging in Publication Data

Berglas, Steven.
  The success syndrome.

  Includes bibliographies and index.
  1. Stress (Psychology) 2. Success—Psychological aspects. 3. Psychotherapy. I. Title.
RC455.4.A87B47   1986                    155.9                    86-15150
ISBN 0-306-42349-9

Plenum Press is a Division of
Plenum Publishing Corporation
233 Spring Street, New York, N.Y. 10013

Printed in the United States of America

For my parents, with love and appreciation for all they have given me.

S.B.

# PREFACE

This book has been divided into four parts that correspond to distinct components of The Success Syndrome. Part One will present a broad-based definition of success and of the luxuries it provides, and a discussion of how certain individuals manage to enjoy it more than others. Part Two begins with a discussion of the stress inherent in success and continues to present a detailed analysis of how The Success Syndrome develops. In Part Three, I will explore some of the more recognizable psychological disorders that The Success Syndrome precipitates. Finally, in Part Four, I will examine the essential clinical features of my Executive Stress Clinic—a therapeutic program for individuals who suffer from The Success Syndrome—and then consider how entire corporations can be adversely affected by success.

Success *should* be a gratifying and enriching experience—in more ways than one. Although in the pages that follow the aversive experiences that can result from success are described in detail, an overriding aim of this book is to enable those who achieve success to enjoy it to the fullest extent possible.

Most of the case histories and examples of The Success Syndrome employed in this book utilize individuals from the Boston or New York area. This should not be construed as indicating that The Success Syndrome is an "East Coast" phenomenon; it affects men and women throughout the nation. My reliance on a restricted sample of individuals and sources to demonstrate various aspects of The Success

Syndrome reflects the fact that I live and work in Boston, and when I read a morning paper, it's either *The New York Times* or *The Boston Globe.*

Steven Berglas

# ACKNOWLEDGMENTS

Several people gave of themselves to facilitate my work on this project. I would like to express my indebtedness to them.

Richard Landau, as he has since 1979, added his brilliant touch to my writing. Despite the demands of his adorable infant daughter and newborn law career, he found the time to make an invaluable contribution to this book. More important, he has my special thanks for being a trusted and supportive ally.

Although the core components of the book—my research on self-handicapping behavior and the clinical program I designed for patients stressed by success—dominated my attention for years, were it not for Barrie Greiff this might still be a "work in progress." I truly appreciate his sound advice and unfailing support, and want to thank him again for a most fateful breakfast.

Gerry Adler, David Boyle, Susan Duffy, Roger and Ellen Golde, Phil Levendusky, Claudia Vocino Landau, Michael Sandler, Len and Marion Saxe, Betsy Sheffer, Patricia Vantine, and Norman Zinberg have my thanks for helping me with various aspects of initiating or executing this project. In addition, I feel fortunate to have been employed as Vice President for Research and Social Programs by the Addiction Recovery Corporation while writing this book.

My sincere appreciation goes to Bob Lobel, Norman Rabb, Derek Sanderson, and Dan Scoggin for lending their respected names and experience of success to this book.

They all did me favors and never asked for a single thing in return.

Last, but definitely not least, I want to thank my editor, Linda Regan, for her genuine concern about this book, obvious technical skills, willingness to bend and break rules for me, and especially for her understanding of The Success Syndrome.

S.B.

# CONTENTS

# INTRODUCTION

*Can success change the human mechanism so completely between one dawn and another? Can it make one feel taller, more alive, handsomer, uncommonly gifted and indomitably secure with certainty that this is the way life will always be? It can and it does!*

Moss Hart

How eloquently the playwright Moss Hart captured the prevailing opinion regarding the impact of success upon self-esteem. No wonder Fortune 500 firms spend thousands upon thousands of dollars on consultants and training programs designed to identify top achievers who are, by their psychological makeup, driven to achieve success. The success-conscious *Zeitgeist* of the 1980s has also spawned a new breed of advisor: Image consultants and a variety of communication-skills trainers who counsel upwardly mobile professionals in techniques that will provide them with the "presence" or "look" of success and the competence so crucial for achieving actual success.[1]

And why not? Who would not want the confidence, security, and *joie de vivre* that derive from success? Beyond building up self-esteem and confidence, there are a myriad of more tangible benefits that are afforded the successful: goods, services, power, status, and even good health. Whereas it was once assumed that developing ulcers was a prerequisite to holding executive positions in business, research now shows that those who work for the power-holders, not the guys in charge, are the Maalox addicts. Add to this the documented finding that achieving success or holding a position of power makes one appear sexier, and you can begin to realize in how many different ways the quality of one's life is improved as a consequence of being successful.

In an essay written 18 months before his death, another famous American playwright, Tennessee Williams, described his reactions to the great success that followed the production of his critically acclaimed *The Glass Menagerie:*

> This winter marked the third anniversary of the Chicago opening of "The Glass Menagerie," an event that terminated one part of my life and began another about as different in all external circumstances as could well be imagined. I was snatched out of virtual oblivion and thrust into sudden prominence, and from the precarious tenancy of furnished rooms about the country I was removed to a first-class room in a Manhattan hotel. . . . This was security at last.
>
> I sat down and looked about me *and was suddenly very depressed.* . . .
>
> I soon found myself becoming indifferent to people. A well of cynicism rose in me. . . . Sincerity and kindliness seemed to have gone out of my friends' voices. I suspected them of hypocrisy. . . . I was impatient of what I took to be inane flattery.
>
> I got so sick of hearing people say, "I loved your play!" that I could not say thank you any more. I no longer felt any pride in the play itself but began to dislike it, probably because I felt too lifeless ever to create another.
>
> *Security is a kind of death, I think, and it can come to you in a storm of royalty checks beside a kidney-shaped pool in Beverly Hills. . . . Ask anyone who has experienced the kind of success I'm talking about—What good is it? Perhaps to get an honest answer you will have to give him a shot of truth serum but the*

*word he will finally groan is unprintable in genteel publications*
[emphasis added].[2]

The contrast of the perspectives offered by Williams and Hart becomes obvious upon learning the title of Williams's essay: "The Catastrophe of Success." While Hart construed success to be a mechanism that changed life so as to *enhance* feelings of security—a cherished outcome—Williams viewed the security deriving from success as "a kind of death"; he even came to disdain the very play that brought him success. Beyond the fact that both Hart and Williams maintained that success could drastically change one's life, their perspectives have nothing in common. The precise *nature* of the change one could expect to experience as a consequence of success varies greatly depending upon which playwright one would identify with. In light of their divergent perspectives, one is left wondering if Hart and Williams really shared a common experience of this thing called success.

In point of fact they did. As we shall see, success is a two-edged sword that can as readily sever trust and interpersonal ties as enable an individual to cut a pathway to a glorious life. More important, the pages that follow will examine the factors that determine which cutting edge of success one will experience.

I intend, throughout this book, to analyze the positive and negative consequences of success, as well as the combination of factors that will determine whether an individual derives gifts and gratifications or suffers despondency and deprivation after reaching "the top." By demonstrating how every imaginable type of success—business, recreational, interpersonal—can prove to be either a blessing or a burden, I hope to clarify the paradoxical aspects of success—the one life experience that most Americans strive to attain, but many fail truly to enjoy. In fact, a realization that feelings of joy and personal satisfaction that follow success are fleeting epitomizes the disorders associated with The Success Syndrome.

The Success Syndrome refers to the positive *and* negative outcomes that follow the attainment of a significant achievement, victory, or goal. When an individual is successful, he* is rewarded with material wealth, fame, prestige, power, control, and influence. However, he is *simultaneously* subjected to a variety of burdensome expectations. On the one hand, a successful person is expected to perform at ever-increasing levels of proficiency each and every time he succeeds. Unless he sustains top-level performances over time, a once-successful person will appear to have failed.

On the other hand, a second type of burdensome expectation imposed on those who succeed involves their obligations to others. A successful person is expected to demonstrate a limitless amount of largess to whomever he encounters, either in terms of direct "giving" or through the willingness to nurture the careers of those who have yet to "arrive." The person who has achieved a significant goal is also expected to tolerate the envy of those he has surpassed en route to "the top"—a task that may be the most demanding of all those imposed upon the successful.

The Success Syndrome can be identified as the condition that develops when the rewards of success expose an individual to a variety of psychologically stressful situations; these render him vulnerable to disorders ranging from depression and drug abuse to self-inflicted failures and even suicide. The cruel paradox of this syndrome is that at the very moment a successful person should be

---

* Throughout this book I employ the masculine form for pronouns purely as a literary convenience. Both sexes are equally capable of achieving success and of falling victim to The Success Syndrome.

enjoying the fruits of his labors, he becomes susceptible to distress he would not have been exposed to were he not successful.

The psychiatric disorders suffered by victims of The Success Syndrome are not necessarily unique. For example, the interpersonal jealousies and mistrust that commonly hack away at the multitude of pleasures promised by success can affect any of us. These, in turn, can precipitate severe mood disturbances such as anxiety or depression. The distinctive feature of an individual who is victimized by The Success Syndrome is the *causal link* between his experience of success and his subsequent suffering.

Although psychological syndromes are harder to document than those involving physiological phenomena, psychiatrists and psychologists continually observe diseaselike syndromes in their patients. Many clinicians still express wonderment when they encounter a patient who "has it all" and fails to enjoy any of it. Yet most therapists recognize that people suffering from The Success Syndrome are found in all age groups, among both sexes, and in every walk of life. My clinical practice has included over the years business executives, physicians, attorneys, professional and teenaged sports champions, and politicians, all of whom suffered from this syndrome. Consider some of the following, more salient examples of people, real and fictional, who have suffered The Success Syndrome.

Few people embody the American ideal of success as do corporate chief executive officers. Not surprisingly, because of the enormous success they have achieved, these men and women are exceptionally vulnerable to The Success Syndrome. According to a story about the life of Hicks Waldron, chief executive officer of Avon Products Inc., the world's biggest beauty-products company, success pro-

vided this man, and others like him, with a host of blessings *and* burdens:

> . . . the reputations of . . . chief executives [have re-
> cently] taken on . . . Protean proportions. There's the
> Croesian salary (often running in the high six-fig-
> ures) . . . the lavish executive suite . . . the limou-
> sines . . . the private jet . . . the power . . . the pres-
> tige. . . .
> For all the glitter and seeming invincibility, though,
> with the job comes almost unending stress. Like his fellow
> C.E.O.'s, Hicks Waldron lives and dies by quarterly num-
> bers and daily stock prices. Poor earnings can quickly leave
> him an ex-C.E.O. He must make crucial decisions based
> on information passed on to him by underlings without
> being certain that it is accurate. . . . His personal wealth
> and position make him and his family vulnerable to kid-
> nappers and other criminal elements. [3]

America's astronauts are undoubtedly considered to
be modern heroes, reaping numerous benefits from their
successful space flights years after they have landed. Some
succeed in being elected to powerful public offices, while
others become presidents of large corporations. For others
less suited to sustaining success, the return to "earthly"
pursuits following success in space is anything but rewarding. Buzz Aldrin, for example, the second man to
walk on the moon, checked into a psychiatric hospital on
the verge of a nervous breakdown within two years after
his successful mission, later admitting that he was a "recovered alcoholic."[4]

The advertising media—who always reflect the latest
trends—have provided us with numerous examples of individuals suffering from success. Who can forget the TV
commercial of the designer of the B.F. Goodrich 721 radial
tire despairing after his office cleaning woman confronts

him with: "So what are you gonna do next?" In a similar vein, recall the televised boardroom where a senior executive reports the previous quarter's *increased* sales/profit figures. Though the news is good, we see pencils breaking, brows wiped of sweat, and Alka Seltzer tablets dropping into water to provide those businessmen with relief from "the stress of success."

In all spheres of life, the effects of The Success Syndrome are being felt. Psychiatrists and psychologists have become regular contributors to such publications as *The Harvard Business Review*, arguing that psychological distress among successful executives can be linked, in certain instances, to the attainment of their goals. They report the symptoms of loneliness and marital breakups with an alarming regularity among supersuccessful business people.[5] One survey appearing in *The Harvard Business Review* reported that business ownership is one of the most satisfying career experiences in American life. Nevertheless, researchers found that "entrepreneurs pay an extremely high cost for such satisfaction—at least once a week 55% to 65% of those surveyed have back problems, indigestion, insomnia, or headaches."[6]

*The New York Times* has also published columns describing consequences of The Success Syndrome. Several years ago, columnist Robert Vare identified a tactic of many Americans seeking a feeling of well-being. As Vare saw it, their serenity was derived from "Avoiding Success":

> Once, in a simpler time, success meant wealth, fame and recognition from one's peers. Today, the recognition is more likely to come from dogged I.R.S. agents, overreaching decorators, cunning kidnappers and hyperactive palimony lawyers. Studies show that nine out of 10 Americans will give up wealth and fame in exchange for legal immunity from Marvin Mitchelson.[7]

Many people who achieve success are incapable of accepting its riches, feeling crippled by the expectations derived from it. My laboratory research has demonstrated an undeniable causal link between certain types of success and alcohol abuse; moreover, in my clinical practice I have seen victims of success destroy their physical health, family life, and careers. I have treated a great many patients who suffered from success and, fortunately, prevailed to return to productive and happy lives.

Using actual first-person reports as well as research and clinical data, this book will analyze the paths that a variety of successful people have followed to arrive "at the top." It will also trace their subsequent descent to despair greater than they had ever known before. My purpose is to identify the psychological factors that sabotage the riches (both material and interpersonal) derived from success, and to provide steps to ensure that success will mean happiness to those who achieve it.

If you are looking for a book that will teach you the procedures necessary to *achieve* success, I suggest *The Way to Wealth* by the articulate businessman/scientist/statesman Benjamin Franklin.[8] *The Success Syndrome* is more of a guide for the individual who is successful, or soon-to-be, and intent upon traveling the road to success with the least cost and most enjoyable accommodations awaiting him. Whether this is your first or final trip toward your personal goal of success, this book will pinpoint how to avoid the pitfalls and maximize the benefits that are potentially yours.

Part One

# SUCCESS: WHAT IT IS; WHAT IT PROVIDES; HOW TO ENJOY IT

Chapter One

# AMERICA'S OBSESSION WITH SUCCESS

*Be all that you can be.*
> U.S. Army recruiting slogan, circa 1984

*You can have it all.*
> Michelob Light advertising slogan, circa 1984

There was a time, not that long ago, when a stern, almost glowering Uncle Sam would peer out at American males from beneath a red-white-and-blue striped top hat and declare, "I Want YOU." This was once an effective means of persuading volunteers to sign up for military service. Not today. Now, even the United States military must promise success, along with glorious future opportunities for self-fulfillment, in appeals for enlistees. Likewise with American breweries. Instead of hawking their particular brand of beer by extolling *its* virtues—remember when advertising used to claim that Budweiser was "The King of Beers" and Miller "The Champagne of Bottled Beer"?— we are now led to believe that certain beverages are the appropriate refreshment for those who have achieved, or are still climbing the ladder toward, success. One Michelob ad campaign of the 1980s explicitly targeted its promotions to success-minded drinkers. Its catch phrase: "You're on the way to the top."

Given that the preceding ads are typical of campaigns currently in vogue on Madison Avenue—the street with its hand on the pulse of the nation—we can see that an obsession with success exists in America. Slogans saluting success are popular with marketing executives because research has documented the consumer's desire to "have it all." Everywhere you turn a wave of ad campaigns for products ranging from sneakers to sunglasses maintain that they can provide *the* missing ingredient to ensure a competitive edge in the chase for success. Vantage Cigarettes promise "the taste of success." A nose spray—Nostrilla—touts itself as providing "the sweet smell of success." As an active participant in the advertising game of one-upmanship, Hilton Hotels has found a way to outdo would-be competitors who merely promise success. Their claim is that they are America's business address because they give *meaning* to success.

At face value, Hilton's ad campaign makes sense. Everybody knows what success is and what gives it meaning. Or do we? Dictionary definitions of "success" emphasize aspects of its meaning that refer to obtaining a desired outcome. You are successful if you get what you want or what you intend. Yet even dictionaries, in their secondary and tertiary definitions, recognize that success implies a degree of worldly prosperity or, to put it simply, wealth and fame. Success, in America, is more than merely attaining what one wants; it is attaining a desired outcome that provides both a high level of material wealth and public recognition.

The most unique aspect of the American perception of success pertains to its *purported* effects on the self-image of those who attain it. Success appears to be an end in its own right. It is the single outcome or result, as Christoper Lasch notes, that in and of itself has the capacity to instill a sense of self-approval.[1] In our culture, there is an inherent worth and merit to beating out the competition, rising to the top, distancing one's self from the "also-rans," and becoming number 1. Our nation has bought the perspective of football immortal Vince Lombardi, who said, "Winning isn't everything, it's the *only* thing."

This national preoccupation with success is evident in business, politics, interpersonal relationships, and athletics. Watch the crowd at any sporting event as television cameras pan the arena. You will see thousands of screaming people proclaiming—supposedly for their team—"We're number 1." In point of fact, a good number of those fans could care less about the team competition going on in front of them, not to mention that their assertion of supremacy is typically inaccurate. What matters to them and the majority of Americans, is that they find some arena in life—at home, work, clubs, sporting events, or taverns—to assert their wish for, or belief in, a number 1 status.

The fact that Americans are no longer motivated simply to "keep up with the Joneses," but instead are intent upon surpassing them, creates a variety of problems for those striving to become number 1. At a minimum, the number of number 1's that can exist is finite; there are a limited number of ladders to success one can climb. This is probably one explanation for the current wave of maniacal identification with sports teams and masses of fans asserting they are number 1. If the Boston Celtics are "your" team and they win the championship to become number 1, by identifying with the city and the team you gain some sense of being number 1 as well.

More important, those who have on their own made it to "the top" may find that the people they surpassed are bitter—now that success is such a national obsession. The successful have gone beyond merely achieving a goal in the eyes of covetous onlookers; they have raised themselves to a more desired level of existence. Although the human emotions of jealousy and envy are as old as mankind, the level of hostility that is often directed at "a success" is greater now than would have been the case when being on a par with one's upwardly mobile neighbors was sufficient cause for happiness.

One explanation offered for the intensified success-striving apparent today is purely economic: there have been two severe recessions since the start of the 1980s. Even the casual observer who contrasts the current national mood with that manifest in the Vietnam era would notice the rise in materialism. Psychologist Dr. Harry Levinson noted, "There had been a tempering of the pursuit of materialism until the recession hit. . . . Now, there is much more of a sense of competition which becomes more intense when those who aren't making it see others buying big cars, starting individual retirement accounts and traveling abroad."[2]

Our current national obsession with success is not a consequence of Americans recently acquiring the notion of competing for success; upward mobility is part of the American Dream. The problem is that we have focused to a greater extent on the material consequences of success than ever before. In a sense, the American notion of *success* is stable and healthy. Our attitudes about *wealth* have shifted somewhat.

Echoing this opinion in a stimulating essay about the rich—most, but not all, of whom are successful—writer Anthony Brandt agrees with Hemingway: the rich are no different from you and me, they simply have more money. Brandt goes on to encapsulate the prevailing opinion of those who have made it, by those who have not:

It's our ambivalence about people with money that makes us think they're different. On the one hand we envy and admire them and devour information about how they live their lives and what they're really like. On the other hand we despise them, we see them as no better than the rest of us and undeserving of special consideration, and it secretly delights us when they go broke or wind up in jail or suffer some other diaster.[3]

And suffer they do. Both the merely rich, and the rich and successful, suffer a host of difficulties just like you and I do. Furthermore, they suffer in unique ways that are a direct effect of The Success Syndrome. To cite just one example, experimental research that I conducted demonstrated that certain types of success can lead to the development of alcohol abuse and alcoholism.[4]

Yet despite an awareness on the part of the upwardly mobile that success has its "price" and that there are risks involved, they do little to alter their behavior to a course other than the path to success. Our national obsession with success is so single-minded that the advertising industry can even exploit the *down* side of success in marketing campaigns without fear of arousing anxiety in their target markets.

In the Introduction, I recalled the advertising campaigns for Alka Seltzer and the Goodrich 721 radial tire that linked those products to the stresses inherent in repeating success. Sero, the company that bills itself as "the last of the great shirtmakers," ran an ad campaign touting its "Suprox" Oxford as being built "to take the stress of success." More recently, TWA and the American Express Card teamed up to publicize first-class travel to Europe. The hook used to snag readers' attention was a photo of a smiling, contented, well-dressed man, fully reclined with a glass of wine, beneath a caption that read: "Ahh. It's Lonely At The Top."

The message of these ad campaigns seems clear: "Who cares about the fact that success causes stress and loneliness? Isn't being number 1 worth the price you have to pay once you get there?" Another hidden message that has spread across the country in campaigns such as TWA's is that the rewards of success, particularly money, can offset all ills resulting from success.

The 1980s is not the first time that success has been recognized as taking a toll on interpersonal relationships or physical health. The 1950s gave us the proverbial "Man in the Gray Flannel Suit," frequently portrayed as a success wracked by ulcers. Yet the difference between the 1950s response to The Success Syndrome and the one that is observable today is that the current ethos supports the notion that the *stress* of success can be alleviated by exploiting the many luxuries afforded by success. The truth is that the denial and distortion of real problems arising from success can lead to many psychological disorders. In simpler terms, people are hitting bottom when they reach the top because of their myopic focus on the rewards at the top as opposed to the full picture.

One group of Americans most representative of the perspective that the rewards of success more than compensate for any problems it may cause are the yuppies (young, upwardly mobile professionals). These men and women, in stark contrast to their drab 1950s male counterparts in gray flannel suits, are notorious for indulging themselves with all the material rewards that success can buy. After the news media lavished inordinate attention on this group's conspicuous indulgences, Newsweek dubbed 1984 the year of the yuppie.[5] In their 15-page special report on these success-seekers, Newsweek identified yuppies as the social class that "lives to buy." Management consultant Dr. Rosabeth Moss Kanter went so far as to say the yuppies are known "not so much by their willingness to work hard for the corporation, but their devotion to accumulating power and getting rich."[6]

Kanter's comments underscore what is most notice-able and most disquieting about America's most recent obsession with success. On the one hand, yuppies—the standard-bearers of the decade—do work long and hard to achieve success. However, on the other hand, their vocational triumphs smack of conspicuous consumption. Viewed from a benign perspective, the yuppie's obsession with success is like a caricature of the way in which Americans define success. Seen with a jaundiced eye, their preoccupation with material rewards is unhealthy.

One 28-year-old female attorney interviewed for the *Newsweek* article maintained that a yearly income of $200,000 would keep her "comfortable" enough to be able to travel and buy the clothes she'd want—two new outfits a week. She added, "The way you look is very important. . . . Sometimes I think it is more important than what you can do."[7] Another "yuppie" woman interviewed in the same article had a kitchen stocked with esoterica that would impress Julia Child. Fondling a prized Perrier Jouet from her 180-bottle collection of wine and champagne she said, "I guess this is a substitute for children."[8]

This national obsession with success and the acqui-sition of its trappings extends far beyond the adult prod-ucts of the baby boom. At the start of the 1980s *U.S. News & World Report* proclaimed that the chase for success has again become a consuming American passion, and we are putting a "renewed emphasis on money and status."[9] A more recent cover story of theirs, which described the ways in which Americans are currently pursuing happiness, in-cluded a section entitled, "Thirst for Success."[10] Accord-ing to one expert who feels that the 60-hour workweek is now commonplace among top executives, "The drive for success is back in style again."[11] This executive recruiter goes on to note that the busy people he's familiar with derive great satisfaction from their long hours on the job:

"It's the thrill of the chase, keeping the score card, the feeling of having influence and power and being able to guide those under them . . ." that presumably counterbalances the strain of 12-hour workdays.

While some might debate whether the current obsession with success is more or less intense than the "gray flannel" years of the 1950s, it is undeniable that in every corner of society people are searching for a way to make it big. As *U.S. News & World Report* notes, the publishing business recently discovered a rival for diet books: howto books of the 1980s with titles such as *Getting Yours, Winning With Deception and Bluff,* and *How to Get Ahead by "Psyching Out" Your Boss and Co-workers.*[12] At the start of this decade, a *Boston Globe* columnist observed: "On the best-seller lists the books on how to flatten your stomach are being replaced by books on how to increase your Krugerrands."[13] And should anyone assume that the 1980s pursuit of success parallels the "gray flannel" decade in being restricted to *the man* who wears the suit, a Gallup/*Wall Street Journal* poll reports that women have definitely been bitten by the success bug: 75% of the female executives polled in the survey reported not taking a hiatus from their jobs for family reasons, while 33% of those in the "young-achiever category"—women under 40 who earn at least $60,000—have no plans for taking time away from their 60-hour workweeks to raise a family.[14]

## WHAT DOES IT ALL MEAN?

There is no simple explanation to account for why workaholism in pursuit of material wealth has currently reached epidemic proportions. Nor is there a way to account for why many women are replacing families and children with 60-hour workweeks and prized bottles of wine. It is, however, relatively easy to detect the fact that although the "me" generation has been transformed into the "my" generation ("my Mercedes, my Rolex, my investment counselor," and so on), they have not achieved more satisfaction than they did when singing peace songs and protesting the war in Vietnam.

Government surveys indicate that most cocaine abuse occurs among affluent males in their middle to late thirties; divorce among that age group occurs in more than 50% of the marriages; and psychotherapists like myself who specialize in executive or corporate stress have a mushrooming pool of referrals. Many still believe the myth that material wealth born of success has a curative potential. This credo survives despite the prevalence of distress among the ranks of those who keep the faith. To make matters worse, the keepers of the faith are rapidly losing sight of what actually constitutes a success.

A number of social critics have noted that America's success-worshiping has gotten out of hand. Social historian Barbara Goldsmith has observed that, as of late, the spotlight and glamour of celebrity status have outstripped merely winning or achieving as the goals of those striving to succeed:

> Many people wish to be admired, not respected, to be perceived as successful and glamourous, not as hardworking and righteous. Among the worthy now are synthetic celebrities, famed for their images not their deeds. They need not have a sense of moral or ethical obligation, and often use our approbation for their own cynical purposes.[15]

While Goldsmith sees "synthetic celebrities" deficit in a moral sense, other commentators maintain that the success-striving that typifies our nation might be best described as a cultural disease.

According to Christopher Lasch, this is certainly the case. In his book *The Culture of Narcissism*, he maintains that the new societal enchantment is self-involvement. In conjunction with our self-absorption (which he defines as narcissism), Lasch, like Goldsmith, finds an exaggerated concern with being viewed as a success as opposed to achieving success. Drawing from the literature dealing with the psychology of corporate management, he concludes:

> The new ideal of success has no content. . . . Success equals success. Note the convergence between success in business and celebrity in politics or the world of entertainment, which also depends on "visibility" and "charisma" and can only be defined as itself. The only important attribute of celebrity is that it is celebrated; no one can say why.[16]

Maybe it was comedian Billy Crystal, former star of NBC-TV's *Saturday Night Live*, who best captured America's obsession with success. Playing the Latin sycophant Fernando, he coined two phrases that may come to be remembered as the slogans of the decade dominated by yuppies: "You look maaahvelous" and "Remember, it is better to look good than to feel good."

Despite being far too old to be a yuppie, and obviously not an American by birth, Fernando is the prototype of the yuppie culture. Dressed for success and ever image-conscious, he *appears* to be on the cutting edge of stardom in his field. But as Crystal winked at the audience, we all knew that there was something fundamentally wrong with Fernando. The core was gone or was never there to begin with. He's pushing too hard; protesting too much. He lives the life-style of the rich and famous, but we wonder, as he repeats and repeats his motto: who is he trying to convince? Is Fernando, the quintessential "beautiful person," souring on the life-style?

Is our concern with success and what it buys a disease of self-absorption? Have our business executives over-dosed on Dale Carnegie's *How to Win Friends and Influence People* and lost the capacity to know the joy of truly caring for others? Will the yuppie ethos overrun our nation, rendering us little more than workaholic hedonists rushing (in Reeboks) from a 12-hour workday to feasts with the proper wine at every course? Probably not. Americans have seen the pendulum of national consciousness swing between extremes of social awareness and hedonistic materialism since our country's inception. History tells us that yuppies will develop some social sensitivity sooner or later. Yet despite this fact, there are important questions that have remained unanswered during times of worshiping the "bitch goddess, success": What are the psychological consequences of our national passion for success on the lives of those who pursue it? Do we really know what happens to those who make it to where they're headed once they get there?

Many who reach "the top" will get the cold beer that Michelob promised along with a host of other rewards. Others get the same rewards and much more than they asked for: they become alcoholics.[17] Many successes who can "hold" their liquor suffer other consequences of The Success Syndrome ranging from failed careers to destroyed relationships.

Once success is attained, long-term joy or a peaceful respite to enjoy the fruits of one's labors is *not* assured. Often, the most apparent consequence of success is the psychological pressure to achieve even greater successes. Many people who achieve success report feeling like the ill-fated king of Greek mythology, Sisyphus, who was doomed to an eternity of scaling the same mountain pushing a stone.

And what about the rewards of success? Does driving

to work surrounded by $48,000 worth of German engi-
neering compensate for 12 hours on the job 6 days a week?
What is the cost of staying at the top in terms of friendships
and one's love life? Is the loneliness that purportedly exists
"at the top" a solitude that one seeks for peace of mind,
or an ostracism that negates the joy of becoming number
1?

Striving for success is currently a national obsession
that no one can deny regardless of how one views it. With
yuppies setting the trend for the country as a whole, some
social critics assert that we have acquired a new materialism that smacks of a social disease. With our hunger for
success currently at an all-time high, we may assume that
the pressures to stay "at the top" for those who arrive are
comparably intense. So too the questions of where to go,
what to do, and what it means if and when you become
number 1. To find answers to these questions, we must
first more fully explore the complex meaning of success.

## Chapter Two

# EXPANDING THE DEFINITION OF SUCCESS

*All excellent things are as difficult as they are rare.*
                                        Spinoza


*There could be no honor in a sure success. . . .*
                                        T. E. Lawrence

"WHOEVER HAS THE MOST TOYS WHEN HE DIES, WINS" reads a T-shirt that is extremely popular with the membership of a prestigious, exclusive men's health club. The businessmen, doctors, and lawyers who sport these shirts are regularly accused of acting like immature boys—advertising their endorsement of a materialistic world-view, more appropriate to a sandbox than an executive suite. Yet few of these men would deny their privately held belief that the extent of one's material holdings *relative to one's peers* is the dominant, if not sole, determinant of success.

The definition of success employed in this book is quite consistent with the message expressed on this provocative T-shirt. On the one hand, success connotes a comparison or ranking that is central to its meaning. Evaluating a person or event as "successful" indicates that the person or event has more of a desired attribute than persons or events in its class. Moreover, claiming that someone is a success tells you something about how that person behaves or has behaved in the past. It tells you that he has previously been credited with a behavior or performance that ranked higher than that of his competitors.

On the other hand, it is undeniable that for most Americans success means possessing money, riches, and luxuries. This perspective is rarely advocated publicly except by those who do it with tongue in cheek or provocative T-shirts. Personal charge accounts at the shops on Rodeo Drive are as regularly laughed at as they are longed for. And many of us smirk knowingly when we hear "ignorant" people ask, "If you're so smart, how come you're not rich?" Yet few would privately fail to acknowledge that there is some fundamental validity in such inquiries. Although there are significant exceptions to this principle, success is most frequently defined in terms of the material rewards it can bestow.

Thus, we can see that the message of the T-shirt presents a fairly accurate reflection of how many people view success. In fact, many academics define success in comparative terms ("whoever has the most toys"), particularly psychologists who investigate and describe how people form judgments of ability, achievement, and success. This body of literature, called "social comparison theory,"[1] holds that everyone has a basic need for self-evaluation (to know "how good they are"). Psychologists maintain that one of the best sources of information capable of satisfying this need derives from comparing one's performances with those of similar individuals. Although determining the "winner" on the basis of who has the most toys may seem overly simplistic and shallow, it is, nevertheless, a psychologically well-grounded approach.

As children, the theory goes, we could determine if we were fast or strong only by competing in races or lifting contests with other children. The winners of such competitions, having compared their abilities with their peers, could be certain that, at a minimum, they were *relatively* able. They would also feel the satisfaction of being successful in having bested the efforts of other competitors who presumably had a fair chance of winning. It is noteworthy that comparisons with playmates who are physically inferior (due to sex or age differences) do not provide the same satisfaction even if the outcome (winning) is the same.

The attributes that are measured when defining success change as we grow older. At cocktail parties the question of who's wealthier than whom is a frequent topic of conversation; who's faster or stronger is not. The process of determining ability and success, however, remains basically the same over time. Success is relative. The judgment that someone is successful is not possible without comparing that individual's performance, resources, or social recognition to that of others with a comparable genetic and socioeconomic background.

This particular approach to defining success is based upon what I refer to as *rewards and superior ranking*. In many ways it is the only way in which successful people can be differentiated from those who are merely rich. Individuals with certain careers can expect rewards as an inherent part of their profession. For instance, international investment bankers will typically earn six-figure salaries. Although most international investment bankers may be *rich*, to be considered successful their income must be compared to others within the investment banking community. An executive secretary who earned $90,000 per year would be judged very successful, whereas an international investment banker drawing the same salary could easily be considered a financial failure.

Historian Richard Huber, in his book about success, expanded the definition of the term beyond a comparison of rewards and ranking within one's peer group:

> What is success? In America, success has meant making money and translating it into status, or becoming fa-

mous. . . . Success was brutally objective and impersonal.
It recorded a change in rank, the upgrading of a person in
relation to others by the unequal distribution of money and
power, prestige and fame. Yet, success was not simply
*being* rich or famous. It meant *attaining* riches or *achieving*
fame. You had to know where a man began and where he
ended in order to determine how far he had come.

How high did one have to rise to be judged a success? . . . [One] measurement of success was having substantially a better job or making more money at the end of
your working life than at the beginning.[2]


To be a success in America, an individual needs to
have achieved more than outdistancing his peers. There
must be some demonstration that a person did something
to attain greater rewards and higher ranking than would
be expected from someone with a comparable "start" in
life. In essence, to be a success an individual must outdis-
tance his parents' economic status or life-style, since it is
their standard of living that really defines where one begins his climb to "the top." As Michael Korda wrote of
success: "It is the distance between one's origins and one's
final achievement. . . ."[3]

With keen insight into the psyche of the American
business and political communities, Korda notes that the
prototypic example of the American tendency to define
success in this manner is symbolized in the political biography containing the slogan, "From log cabin to the
White House." One immigrant businessman who made it
to the White House as Secretary of the Treasury and is
now chief executive officer of the Burroughs Corporation,
W. Michael Blumenthal, finds the tradition of defining
success in terms of distance traveled relative to one's parents a singularly American phenomenon: "One of the unique

things about this country is that it's just as much or more of an honor to say, 'My father came steerage from Sicily,' as to say, 'My father's family has been here for twelve generations.' "[4]

Korda's prototypic "log cabin to the White House" biography is deeply embedded in the consciousness of the American political system. So much so that many politicians have taken to manufacturing histories that would permit them to incorporate a myth resembling this biography into their public personae. Several of those who could not convince the electorate that they were part of the national "rag-to-riches" myth (e.g., Nelson Rockefeller) found that their political career suffered significant harm. Wendell Wilkie, in his campaigns against Franklin D. Roosevelt, tried to adopt the public image of a poor boy from humble beginnings. Despite this clever posturing, his political fortunes were damaged severely by Harold Ickes's famous description of him as "the barefoot boy from Wall Street."[5] As an electorate we have a strong tendency to judge the worthiness of politicians on the basis of how they came to acquire their money. Those who typify the "log cabin" myth are accepted with little hesitancy. Acceptance is less forthcoming for those "success stories" who are in some way "handed" good fortune on a silver platter.

One of the first people to perceive the value and utility of denying wealthy origins in favor of adopting a rags-to-riches biography was Benjamin Franklin. His use of strategic *downward* self-promotion, according to Korda, was classic. Franklin, who adopted the pen name of Poor Richard, attempted throughout his writing career to convince his audience that he deserved this moniker. In reality, Franklin was a brilliant businessman who amassed a fortune early in his career. By "pleading poverty," Franklin

was really trying to ensure public acceptance. He hoped
that people would not say of him, as Poor Richard said of
another, "He does not possess wealth, wealth possesses
him."

A number of modern businessmen have recently tried
to follow Franklin's lead. They have sensed the values of
their markets and have presented themselves in a manner
consistent with those groups' needs. One salient example
is Lee Iacocca. In his brilliant Chrysler advertising campaigns and later in his autobiography, Iacocca subtly, and
with the skill of a surgeon, presented himself and his company to the American public as emerging from extremely
unenviable origins. Without belaboring Iacocca's personal
or professional success story, it is apparent that his poor-
mouthing paid off. In 1986 he has often been discussed as
a favored contender for the Democratic Party's 1988 presidential ticket.

With a clear understanding of the strategic value of
Korda's "log cabin" myth in mind, the quote provided
above by T. E. Lawrence becomes clearer. We can now
understand why he maintained that there could be no
honor (satisfaction, joy, or increased self-esteem, for that
matter) from a sure success. Sure successes accrue to those
of noble birth, aided by the wealth of their ancestors. The
road to sure success is covered with a red carpet, which
does not conform to the American ideal of achieved success. Moreover, it's unsatisfying. Like stealing candy from
a baby, the "thief" has the goal in hand, but the sweet
smell and taste of success are absent. Honorable successes,
such as those described in the plots of all Horatio Alger
rags-to-riches novels, emerge from situations within which
nothing is guaranteed; in fact, the odds are against a favorable outcome.

Thus, in understanding the meaning of success, particularly in America, it is important to underscore the significance of succeeding against the odds. Our nation began as an underdog and we are always pulling for whichever David is willing to tackle a waiting Goliath. Americans seem to have a special love for successful people who triumph despite having a handicap. People like George Washington Carver and Helen Keller are enshrined in the national psyche not so much for what they've done but for what they had to overcome to do it. Upon learning that Steven Jobs and Stephen Wozniak began Apple Computer in a garage and went on to succeed in an economic market dominated by IBM (or, as insiders call the giant, "*Big* Blue"), the status afforded their success is far greater than would be the case had they begun working with a grant from AT&T. A general psychological "truth" is contained within a paraphrasing of Spinoza: All worthwhile successes are as difficult as they are rare.

## SILVER SPOONS CAN LEAVE BITTER AFTERTASTES

It is ironic to think that being born into "money," coming from the "right" family, or "having connections" can actually *prevent* a person from becoming a success, but it can and often does. These "head starts" do not necessarily impede one's capacity for securing high-status vocations, gaining a favorable earning potential, or gathering material acquisitions. They do, however, frequently deprive an individual of being *judged* successful. Many of those "born with silver spoons in their mouths" realize that they "have it all," but recognize as well that they did not earn enough of "it" to qualify as a success in the eyes of their peers.

Many of the individuals who fall victim to The Success

Syndrome suffer severe psychological disorders as a result of being trapped and, essentially, damned by their affluent heritage. A 35-year-old patient of mine whose surname is inextricably linked with a highly profitable manufacturing concern has often cursed his name, wishing that he could shed it and the excessive performance standards it imposes on him. As he explained when we first met, "Everyone in my family is expected to succeed because that's what my relatives have been doing since they came to this country. The hard part is that to succeed isn't enough for me and my brother. We've got to *exceed* the family's level of prior successes or people will say that we blew the opportunities we had."

A 24-year-old female patient of mine from another well-known family expressed poignantly the disadvantages of her heritage: "It's bad enough that being a [name] deprived me of receiving full credit for what I did, it was assumed that a [name] would succeed. I think of how horrible it would be to pass this curse along to *my* children. My kids will have a first name plus their father's, none of this using my maiden name as one of theirs. Let them have the benefits of my family's backing wihout the burdens."

This patient is not alone in her concerns. George Pillsbury has developed and leads consciousness-raising groups consisting of people with inherited wealth who, in a style comparable to Alcoholics Anonymous, help each other cope with the burdens of being wealthy heirs. According to one group member, "It's not easy having money. . . . I'm envious, in a way, of friends who don't have inherited wealth."[6]

This dilemma of being born wealthy is but one example of how *ostensibly* beneficial "head starts" can contribute to the experience of The Success Syndrome. Most success-induced disorders that I encounter in my clinical practice derive from the degree of ambiguity inherent in many forms of success. Often, as in the case of heirs to great fortunes, a person's overt performance in a given area may be superior to all competing performances, but may fall short of that which is expected from members of his profession, background (e.g., level of schooling), or family. And as we will explore more fully below, many people who achieve their goals fail to derive feelings of satisfaction because the criteria for determining the number 1 performance are, for the most part, subjective.

When ambiguity and subjective criteria for judging success cloud the meaning of accomplishments that appear to qualify as successes, psychological distress is an inevitable consequence. It is not uncommon to find that individuals who have head starts in life pursue careers in fields unrelated to their backgrounds in order to shed the negative influence of their favorable upbringing. The protagonist in the film *Five Easy Pieces* (played by Jack Nicholson) abandoned a career in classical music, along with his considerable aptitude, rather than labor beneath the burden of his family's heritage of great pianists.

Many others who are "blessed" with head starts react to the ambiguity surrounding their potential successes with more specific symptoms. For example, my research on success-induced alcohol abuse demonstrates that the distress generated by not knowing if one succeeded as a function of one's ability as opposed to luck is enough to motivate many people to drink.[7] One of the more intriguing findings from this research was that when experimental subjects were informed that they had been successful on a task designed explicitly to create an ambiguous success experience, they did not report feeling that their success was in any way tainted or undeserved. Yet these subjects were disturbed enough by ambiguous success feedback to drink, but not to reject receipt of the success. Apparently, given the desirability of success, people will tolerate the stress of being in situations where the meaning of what "should" be a successful performance is in doubt, and find ways to cope with their distress rather than forfeit success.

## TWO QUALIFICATIONS TO THE REWARDS AND RANKING DEFINITION OF SUCCESS

A major problem inherent in the process of determining what is to be judged a success and what is not is that many abilities defy measurement. A person's weight-lifting ability or speed can be appraised directly in terms of an "objective reality," and readily extrapolated across a variety of persons and situations. Barbells can be weighed and races can be timed. Managerial skill, on the other hand—being a more abstract concept—is amorphous and resists traditional forms of measurement. Its assessment relies heavily on the opinions and judgments of others.

There are a variety of desirable attributes and skills, essential for success in business, government, law, medicine, communications, and the like, that cannot be weighed, timed, or measured. Thus, success in these arenas relies heavily on the subjective opinion of a "judge" who may have any number of biases. This subjective quality of judging complicates the process of determining success. Since personal biases are not customarily announced by judges, individuals who fail to become number 1 often feel that they could have achieved success had their efforts been evaluated by a more sympathetic audience.

We often hear that people who achieve success were in the "right place at the right time." The corollary of this key to success is to "pick your spots." Both pieces of business wisdom can be distilled to the core maxim that success is not always an indicator of merit but, at times, of Kismet. A man may create a new idea or product that does not find a receptive market during his lifetime but may sell after his death. Such a person may rate a footnote in history, but could hardly be considered a success. Interestingly, should a sagacious entrepreneur stumble across the same ingenious idea or product, dust it off, and package it anew, he would be given credit for a success if the previously "discovered" idea or product met with unbounded enthusiasm the second time around.

John, Viscount Morley of Blackburn, underscores this complicated problem in his commentary on the origins of success:

> Success depends on three things: who says it, what he says, how he says it; and of these three things, what he says is the least important.[8]

Success may depend upon the transient mood of an evaluator or, worse yet, upon finding the right evaluator to ensure the desired outcome. The direct implication of this observation is that an individual must typically strive for success within the confines of a particular "universe" that is receptive to his unique skills and goals. The concept of casting pearls before swine has particular relevance here: aspirants for a number 1 ranking would do well to consider the context of their performances as carefully as the content of what they present for evaluation.

Many stellar performers and extremely competent performances will not receive the appreciation they are due because they were presented to unsophisticated audiences. For the performer, this is undeniably an extremely painful experience. Yet for many individuals who *do* achieve success precisely because they have had the foresight to choose a receptive audience, the knowledge that they won with what might be construed to be a "stacked deck" has far more potential for psychological damage. To paraphrase the introductory quote from T. E. Lawrence: there could be no honor, peace of mind, or comfort in a sure success.

In our examination of the disorders accompanying The Success Syndrome, we will focus on a number of negative consequences resulting from successes achieved as a result of biased audiences. The political maxim "there's no such thing as a 'free lunch' " has a special meaning for those who achieve "sure" successes. Politicians who accept purportedly "free" lunches are obligated to pay back their benefactors with a variety of political favors that may, if they escalate to true corruption, cost an elected official his career and reputation. Those who accept "sure" successes are also obligated to their audiences and must, like a "bought" politician, live with a degree of anxiety, self-doubt, and guilt, for as long as they see their success as dependent upon the largess of a particular audience. If an audience "giveth," it can "taketh away," an awareness that definitely saps the joy from success and can lead to severe psychological distress.

## THE EXPERIENCE OF SUCCESS FREE FROM AMBIGUITY

When discussing an unqualified success, the kind that Moss Hart claimed changed the "human mechanism" so favorably, we are speaking of an experience that is not so fragile as to depend upon the idiosyncratic assessments of a few people. It must be recognized by the majority of a particular universe—be they members of the American

Kennel Association, the Young Presidents Organization, or the American Psychiatric Association. This majority must be cognizant of the criteria for superior achievement in its particular area of specialization. According to Harold Laski, "The vital roots of the American spirit are either the building of a fortune or the building of a reputation which makes you held in esteem by your neighbors."[9]

An important attribute of success is that it bestows upon the one who achieves it a large measure of *status* and *prestige* by others who can appreciate the feat. For our purposes, status can be understood to mean a top ranking by the spoken consensus of a group concerned with that particular area. The successful person who attains status within his universe is also understood to hold a commensurate degree of prestige—the esteem, respect, or approval that others in his group grant for his superior performance.[10]

This qualification of our original definition of success as a ranking must be taken one step further: the status and prestige of any given "success" depend not only on the ranking of a performance within a universe, but on the ranking of that universe within society-at-large. A district manager employed by IBM is far more successful than the chief executive officer of a one-man vending enterprise. Stated another way, the amount of success an individual can claim and enjoy will vary as a joint function of how big a fish he is and the size of the pool he swims in.

The requirement that a meaningful success be acknowledged by an informed audience that extends beyond an individual's intimate contacts (e.g., family, personal friends) eliminates feelings of ambiguity and distress from sure successes. Although widespread adulation is not synonymous with inherent worth, it does signify a broad base of unbiased support. With some degree of universal support comes the confidence that judgments of success did not come about because of idiosyncratic biases such as those that would arise within restricted audiences. Certain "truths" are derived by consensus, and in many cases "deserved" success is one of them.

The recognition that success provides more than "the almighty dollar" begins to explain why successful people are in such enviable positions. Occasionally successful people possess less cash than others but have more clout, owing to their unique status or prestige. There are a variety of careers or kinds of status that, while highly admired, are not rewarded with material riches. For example, if we compare an archbishop with a lottery winner this assertion becomes obvious. The clergyman has every attribute of success—rank, status, and prestige, and various perks such as luxurious accommodations and access to travel—*except* money, whereas the lottery winner, as far as we know, has no greater claim to fame than the money he derived through good luck.

The one instance in which this argument is regularly confounded or subverted involves discussions of celebrities and notorious figures. Ralph Ross and Ernest van den Haag have maintained, "if Marilyn Monroe has a much larger income than Einstein did—and she has—it is a sign that as a whole we want, or value, her services more than his."[11] Others clearly disagree. Sociologists often note that there are many individuals who have achieved great wealth and yet are often rejected by elite circles for lack of "proper breeding."[12]

In the aggregate, however, the available data seem to suggest that "filthy lucre" is rarely spurned by even the "cleanest" people. There's an American ethic that has made explicit the virtues of amassing as much wealth as possible.[13] As August B. Hollingshead observed following his study of a small Midwestern town in the 1940s: "To be sure, other cultural factors enter the picture, but in this acquisitive, success-dominated ideology the primary criterion of 'social worth' is measured in terms of dollars."[14]

Then how does the archbishop come to enjoy a significant measure of success, replete with status and prestige? To answer this question we return to the definition of success offered earlier by Huber. According to this historian, success meant making money and then *translating* it into status or fame. Acquisition or ranking was only the initial stage of the *process* of becoming successful. As Huber saw it, success meant achieving fame rather than being famous, and the actual goal of the "rags-to-riches" journey was the ascent to respectability: "The process was the translation of an economic class position derived from making money to a social class position which was partially established by the spending of it. It was economic achievement becoming social achievement."[15]

It appears, in the final analysis, that the successful in America comprise a distinct social class. It is a grouping composed of individuals who have achieved a particular type of ranking that usually brings the reward of material riches, and always conveys the attainment of an exalted position in the eyes of their community. Theirs is a prominent, obvious, and envied position in our culture that, like every other social stratum, conveys a set of *rights and obligations* upon occupants of the class. In the pages that follow, it will become apparent that the particular set of rights and obligations bestowed upon the successful are among the primary determinants of the blessings and burdens that comprise The Success Syndrome.

We have examined the defining features of success and found that it implies, first and foremost, a number 1 or superior ranking within a circumscribed universe. In

America, success is most often linked to material rewards. This definition is qualified by an understanding that rankings and rewards that do not elevate an individual to a high social standing of status and prestige *do not* qualify him as a true success.

Another extremely important qualification to our definition of success involves the extent to which an individual is aided versus impeded by external forces in his quest for success. The Horatio Alger, rags-to-riches route to success is the one most respected by Americans. We discovered that head starts and favorably disposed audiences may function as double-edged swords in the lives of those who strive for success. Head starts will typically assure an individual of significant earning potential and access to *opportunities* for success, but may deprive him of *credit* for what he achieves. By the same token, finding or selecting an audience that can be counted on to approve of one's work will guarantee the experience of success. The problem is that "sure" successes are devoid of meaning and, worse yet, typically contribute to the psychological distress deriving from The Success Syndrome.

The successful American has accomplished something putting him in a social class that gives him the freedom to behave in particular ways and requires him to behave in others. The way in which a successful person responds to his rights and obligations as "a success" will determine his ultimate reaction to success—whether he masters or succumbs to The Success Syndrome.

Chapter Three

# SUCCESS

## Happiness and Pleasure

*The things which . . . are esteemed as the greatest good
of all . . . can be reduced to these three things: to wit,
Riches, Fame, and Pleasure.*

Spinoza

*If I were a rich man . . . The most important men in
town would come to call on me . . . They would ask me
to advise them, like a Solomon the Wise . . . Posing
problems that would cross a Rabbi's eyes!*

*And it won't make one bit of difference if I answer right
or wrong . . . when you're rich they think you really
know.*

Tevye from Anatevka (*Fiddler on the Roof*)

Success, as described in the preceding chapter, derives from three interrelated factors: (1) comparative ranking, (2) rewards, especially money, and (3) social status or prestige. Each component of success is valued by our society in and of itself. Winning or being at the top of one's field is satisfying, providing ego gratification or self-pride. Money, according to folk wisdom and the Beatles, can buy virtually anything but love. And status or prestige is like verbal embraces, smiles, and applause all rolled into one positive feeling. In fact, the riches and fame inherent in success account for two-thirds of what Spinoza held was the "greatest good of all." In many instances, success will also lead to the experience of the remaining element in Spinoza's list, pleasure.

Tevye, from *Fiddler on the Roof*, despite never having read Spinoza, knew that riches were a key element of success and of all good things in life. He understood that "important men" would come to call upon the rich and treat them with respect. Tevye knew that despite their importance (derived, presumably, from political clout), these men would confound *his* having money with "really knowing" the answer to virtually any question.

Tune in any talk show and listen to hosts interview actors, athletes, and authors who've made it big. They'll ask them to expound on topics with little or no bearing on their particular area of expertise. Hearing star performers comment on geopolitical affairs or concerns of social science can be quite entertaining, but enlightened audiences should question the amount of *expert* information contained in their remarks. Yet many audience members do give much greater credence to a star's remarks than they would to those of a randomly selected college professor. There's an unshakable belief within the collective psyche of our nation that if you're on the top of the heap in one arena, you can sit atop *any* other heap you choose.

The linkage between money and status in America today is both strong and symmetrical: As riches breed the presumption of wisdom, manifestations of mental excellence breed questions of "where's the cash?" Individuals who achieve honors or accomplish meritorious work in specialized fields such as science or fine arts are often urged by materialistic family or friends to convert at least part of their intellectual brilliance into the "almighty dollar." There must be something lacking somewhere, the reasoning goes, if your achievement isn't worth money on the open market.

The riches and fame connection is so resilient that those who've acquired great wealth through undeniably underhanded or amoral means are judged less harshly by "proper society" than the comparably devious who have failed to convert their illicit behavior into wealth. Consider the following examples of the way in which riches and fame have an impact on the functioning of our criminal justice system:

When the film executive Robert Evans was convicted of cocaine use, his sentence was to create a program to deter young people from using drugs. When the Hollywood studio head David Begelman pleaded no contest to charges of embezzling funds from Columbia Pictures, he was ordered to continue his psychiatric care.

Contrast these sentences to the one given William James Rummel for three nonviolent crimes that netted him a total of $230.11—life imprisonment (a judgment upheld by the Supreme Court).[1]

Certain transgressions of the law are deemed "white-collar" to denote the dress and social station of the criminal as well as the style and status of the crime. Why can celebrated white-collar criminals escape social censure? Because it is presumed that they (rich law-breakers) must have some degree of true intelligence/worth/value underneath their "bad habits" if they have succeeded in rising to white-collar status.

The example of how success influences our assessment of criminal behavior is just one of the many ways in which this embodiment of "the greatest good" influences our perceptions of others' worth. A review of the meaning of celebrity by social historian Barbara Goldsmith echoes this opinion. Today, she argues, the line between those who are famous and infamous is blurred or has been erased. As a nation we regularly exempt the successful who go astray from adhering to hard moral rules. Our current criterion for celebrity is merely that an individual encapsulate some form of the American Dream, including wealth, success, and glamour. Yet even with such a meager standard, America still accords celebrities the substantial rewards once reserved for more deserving heroes: "social acceptance, head-of-the-line access, public acclaim, monetary gains and the ability to influence the power structures and institutions of our nation."[2]

If we review our definition of success alongside the

list of rewards that Goldsmith believes should be accorded America's deserving heroes, Spinoza's notion of the "greatest good," and what Tevye believed would accrue from becoming rich, we see that there are essentially three consequences of success beyond monetary gain. The lives of those who reach "the top" are enriched by: prestige, freedom, and psychological control or power. With no offense to Hilton Hotels intended, these outcomes are what give meaning to success.

## PRESTIGE

In 1984, following the Grammy Awards telecast (dubbed "The Michael Jackson Special" by some), *Tonight Show* host Johnny Carson walked onstage to deliver his monologue wearing one white sequined glove. He has also "moonwalked" for his national audience on more than one occasion. What does this mean? Maybe not much, but Michael Jackson's impact was felt across the nation in a number of other ways between 1983 and 1985: He appeared on the cover of several national magazines, assisted the White House in a campaign against teenage drug abuse, initiated the most overpublicized concert tour in the nation's history, helped to organize a fund-raising campaign against the Ethiopian famine, and made millions upon millions of dollars from his artistically acclaimed songs and videos.

Michael Jackson is a brilliant musician. But as we see from the range of his activities during the mid-1980s, he has been much more than that. His prestige as a rock superstar has influenced the entire country by shaping attitudes, appetites, and trends.

The prestige of Lee Iacocca has had even more of an

impact. Called "An American Legend" and "America's best-known and popularly respected businessman" by *Newsweek*,[3] this author, media pitchman, foundation chairman, corporate president, and CEO is probably one of the most *politically* influential men in America today. As a result of his monumental success at the Ford Motor Company and his rescue of Chrysler Corporation (including the early repayment of a loan in the amount of $813,487,500), his name has been bandied about the corridors of influence in Washington as a possible: (1) running mate for former Democratic presidential candidate Walter Mondale; (2) member of Ronald Reagan's Cabinet; (3) Democratic presidential candidate in 1988. What has been the route to this bipartisan popularity? Prestige derived from success in business! In 1984 his salary and bonus from Chrysler Corporation were estimated to be over $1 million; his book royalties about $4 million; and his personal worth over $20 million.[4]

Prestige can also cover up a multitude (and millions of dollars worth) of sins. Frank Borman, who orbited the moon on the Apollo 8 flight in 1968, is a bona fide American hero. He is also a man who acknowledges that he got the job of president of Eastern Airlines because he is a former astronaut. Despite the fact that Eastern has lost its status as the number one carrier of passengers among American airlines during the first five years of his stewardship, Borman has been able to retain his $282,000-a-year presidency. How can a man with such a lackluster record remain in a leadership position? Prestige. According to one Wall Street analyst who is puzzled by Borman's not being axed at Eastern after posting more than $400 million worth of losses: "Maybe firing him would be like firing Santa Claus."[5]

And then there's what I call the "Tevye effect," a phenomenon I noted earlier of rich and famous people pontificating on subjects that have nothing to do with the acquisition of material wealth or their particular area of expertise, and being judged authoritative or knowledgeable in any and every field. Media-master Iacocca recognizes the confusion that occurs when prestigious performers gain access to the airwaves, and presents a clear understanding of how judgments of competency are blurred through massive public exposure. Iacocca, who believes that he's qualified to assume a Cabinet or a higher government position, apparently feels that public office should result from meritorious performance in related fields of endeavor as opposed to stardom and publicity in the entertainment field. Says the star of Chrysler's TV ad campaign: "Many people think I'm an actor. That's ridiculous. Everybody knows being an actor doesn't qualify you to be President."[6]

Why do Americans have this insatiable desire to identify with the successful, even imitating their dress and style? Why is it that corporations will tolerate substandard performances from celebrity CEOs? And why is it that the combination of wealth and media exposure conveys an air of intelligence and authority? The answer to these questions and an understanding of why prestige enhances the lives of the successful can be found by examining the psychology of what goes on within "the eye of the beholder," or in psychological terms, the study of person perception.

Studies of person perception have yielded a set of rules describing how we come to judge other people as possessing certain attributes, abilities, or traits. Whether the focus is on a person's perceived level of aggressiveness or his worldliness, the rules of person perception are uniform. An examination of two of these rules will help explain why prestige derived from success has such a far-reaching impact.

*Rule No. 1: Exposure Leads to Liking.* Many people are famous for just being famous. They do not have to do anything to achieve a certain level of prestige. Almost anyone who reads the newspaper knows of Princess Diana, Prince Charles, and their two sons. Yet few will be able to list their accomplishments apart from being in line for titles and riches. In the 1980s most royal families are famous simply because of the number of times they have been placed before the public for viewing. It may sound simplistic, but it is a psychological fact: we come to like those things that we are exposed to repeatedly even if our experience with the "exposed" object is completely neutral. Just seeing or hearing a stimulus time and time again leads an individual to prefer that stimulus over other comparable stimuli.[7]

Psychologists have no clear-cut understanding of why this so-called "mere exposure" effect works, but its effectiveness is surely recognized by advertisers and politicians. Consider the popularity of a man like Walter Cronkite, who, when he anchored the *CBS Evening News,* was invariably ranked as being one of the most respected men in the nation. At one point, following his retirement from full-time duties at CBS, he was considered a contender for the 1984 Democratic vice presidential candidacy as well as other elective offices. Although he is unquestionably one of the premier broadcast journalists of all time, at least part of the respect afforded Mr. Cronkite, as well as his appeal as a political candidate, stems from the fact that he was "exposed" to a significant proportion of the nation's TV audience on the network news. Who else has spoken to American families about important events five times a week for decades?

Prestige, like an advertising slogan, keeps a person in the public's eye. Once the public embraces a celebrity, the effect of exposure leading to liking starts to snowball. Most newspapers devote at least one column to "social scene" or gossip items, and some magazines devote themselves almost exclusively to exposing the lives of famous people. As media exposure leads to liking, liking breeds a demand for more exposure (creating and selling more tabloids). The "mere exposure" law might be the reason why celebrity press agents have been known to claim, following a client's bad review: "There's only one thing worse than being written negatively about and that's not being written about at all."

What is certain is that prestige and the exposure it affords the successful account for some of the adulation the successful receive from the public. When celebrities have done something to deserve the exposure (or "ink," as newspaper writers call it), the effect is all the more powerful since competency breeds respect and admiration as well. However, even in the absence of an understanding of what factors warrant prestige, the mere fact that one is presented to the public at frequent intervals makes that person liked by those he is exposed to.

*Rule No. 2: "Innate" Personality Theories Govern Our Judgments of Others.* Whereas the "Golden Rule" advocates that we should do unto others as we would have them do unto us, rules of person perception have proven that what we do unto others depends upon how these others are categorized in our mental coding systems. This is most clearly visible with respect to racist behaviors stemming from categorizing a class of people as "bad" or hated. When a person is characterized as "warm" for example, we expect that interactions with him will be favorable, and thus treat him accordingly. We don't expect warm people to collect past due bills or present us with speeding tickets. Such behaviors are expected from "cold" people. In a similar fashion, we expect academics to be idealistic and have lofty thoughts, while businessmen are expected to be ruthless.

In reality, these expectations are quite often false. The back-stabbing and bitter infighting that go on in The Ivory Tower could make the social climate in many corporate boardrooms seem idyllic. As one professor friend of mine is fond of saying, the political fighting for "turf" in academic departments is so violent precisely because there's little else at stake.

Psychologists have demonstrated that despite glaring exceptions to "the rules," our impressions of others are almost always organized around a central trait or focal attribute. Moreover, additional bits of information that we acquire about a person are not processed in an additive fashion. Instead, characteristics of a person that may actually be quite independent are judged to be highly correlated in the minds of observers. This phenomenon, dubbed the "halo effect,"[8] demonstrates that people build integrated impressions of others on the basis of key traits and their preexisting prejudices.

A series of experiments conducted in 1946 illustrate how the halo effect works. Psychologist Dr. Solomon Asch varied only one term in a list of seven adjectives used to describe a fictional person to groups of experimental subjects. This one change created virtually opposite impressions of the "same" hypothetical person.[9] Dr. Asch referred to the person in question as being intelligent, skillful, industrious, determined, practical, and cautious, in addition to *either* warm or cold. His results were dramatic. The "warm" person was also judged to be happy, generous, humorous, and humane, while the "cold" person was thought to be ungenerous, irritable, humorless, and ruthless.

The Asch investigations provide us wih information

central to an understanding of how the success a person experiences affects the judgments of others. Of greatest importance is the finding that certan traits (e.g., warm versus cold) are central to judgments that we form of others. It has been shown that total impressions of a person may develop quite elaborately from knowledge of only one highly central attribute. Considering America's obsession with success, we can safely assume that "successful" will be one of those "central" traits, like warm or cold, that will exert a directive influence over the entire process of forming impressions of others.

The concept of how central traits influence our judgments of others has been extended by several psychologists who have investigated the operation of *implicit personality theories*.[10] Simply stated, implicit (also called "lay" for layman's) personality theories are the rules that average people use when making judgments of others. Psychologists, who have formalized these rules, note that implicit personality theories extend the clustering influence of central traits to people making judgments of others on the basis of *observing* behavior, rather than being told of a central trait.

For example, if we see an individual on the *Tonight Show* and know nothing about that person except that he or she is the guest of Johnny Carson, implicit personality theories predict that we would be psychologically willing and able to say that we know a great deal about this person. To understand how this "knowledge" emerges, let us examine a typical set of inferences drawn after seeing a previously unknown person as a guest on the *Tonight Show:*

Inference No. 1: The guest is important or noteworthy. Why? Because of the fact that access to the *Tonight Show* is extremely limited. A person must do or be something important or noteworthy to have gained access to this limited resource.

Inference No. 2: The guest is most probably talented. Why? Most of the guests on the *Tonight Show* are accomplished performers, so it's a safe bet (statistically) that this guest is a talented performer as well.

This analysis could be extended through a variety of additional desirable attributes but it would be unnecessary for the lay personality theorist. On the basis of the inferences discussed above, the average person has more than enough information to "know" that the previously unknown guest on the *Tonight Show* is worthy of the social acceptance and public acclaim reserved for prestigious people. Once this knowledge is encoded as a central trait, the *Tonight Show* guest will be viewed as possessing a host of positive attributes typically associated with being a success.

The consequence of this inferential reasoning for those who attain success is quite straightforward: positive judgments associated with success will spread around them like a "halo." They will soon become aware of the fact that other people hold favorable opinions of them that extend far beyond their manifested abilities. As Tevye said, when you're rich they think you really know (and are kind, handsome, and humorous as well).

As many successful people know, the halo of positive expectations derived from success can, occasionally, become a burden rather than a blessing. Many talented performers are unwilling or unable to assume the celebrity status that their success affords them. Being unaccustomed or downright adverse to talking about what they do, some artists, authors, sports figures, and scientists find that they were happier when unknown and unencumbered by the need to assume a range of social skills unrelated to their particular area of expertise. For many superachievers, The Success Syndrome begins when a halo of success takes hold and their anonymity is wrested from their grasp.

An additional consequence of this halo effect is that it grants successful people access to others of comparable status. In politics or business, this positive consequence of success is called the ability to "open doors"; hence, a person who is successful in one field can typically gain access to those who are successful in others. Evidence of this phenomenon is apparent at most "important" White House dinners where "stars" from government, Hollywood, the business community, and the sports world share tables and small talk. As noted earlier, the successful constitute a distinct social class in America, and, virtually without exception, have unlimited access to important people in every other social class. This ability to traverse traditional class lines at will—a social freedom of mobility—is related to a host of other "freedoms" that derive from success.

## FREEDOM

"The promise of Palm Springs has always been escape," is how *Newsweek* began an article about the town it called "an oasis of privacy providing movie stars, gangsters and the merely rich with sanctuary from worldly cares and bad weather."[11] One writer who developed an exhaustive list of "the perquisites of success" typically afforded top executives noted, "Most of these perks have one thing in common: they tend to insulate the successful executive from other people, to smooth and protect his passage through the world."[12]

There is no question that one's passage through the world is made more difficult by bad weather, unruly and obnoxious crowds at theaters and other public places, and the typical worldly cares that hassle all of us. Although philosophers have concluded that the daily distress of life lets us appreciate the good and beautiful, it is safe to say that for those who can afford it, being rid of everyday inconveniences tops their list of ways to spend their money.

Success can provide you with freedom from the daily annoyances of life. You can buy your way to the front of a restaurant line, or to any preferred table for that matter. Success can also buy you the freedom to avoid the drudgery of a disliked job. Benjamin Franklin was initially a very successful businessman. He abandoned the hectic world of work in favor of a relaxed life-style in science and public service despite a virtual certainty that he could have considerably increased his personal fortune had he been so inclined. But beyond an early and leisurely retirement and the privilege of avoiding snowstorms, long lines, and noisy streets, what's so special about the freedom derived from success?

What's special is that freedom from the daily hassles of life has been proven to be good for your psychological and physical well-being. In a word, freedom yields health.

Until recently, informed psychiatric opinion was dominated by the belief that stress and related disorders (e.g., coronary heart disease, hypertension, ulcers) were linked with so-called "major life events."[13] According to this theory, the more major life events that someone had to confront within a given time frame, the more likely that person would suffer some form of psychosomatic disorder. High on this list of the events precipitating disorders caused by stress are death of family members, unfaithfulness of spouses, business and financial reversals, and divorce.

Several different groups of psychiatric researchers, however, are now demonstrating that daily hassles are more likely to cause physical breakdowns than are the major life events. In addition, studies of populations ranging from nurses to bankers have shown that the presence of positive life events (called uplifts) allows people to withstand the trauma of major problems as well as the ravages of daily hassles. A group of researchers from the University of California at Berkeley have quantified hassles (waiting in lines, inconsiderate smokers, traffic jams) as well as uplifts (friendly co-workers, getting a present, completing a task) and have demonstrated a significant positive relationship between exposure to hassles and psychosomatic disorder, and an inverse relationship between uplifts and the damages caused by hassles.[14]

The findings from this body of research are easily translatable into terms that apply to the perks executives derive from organizational rank. Secretaries, assistants, private cars, dining rooms, and the like can now be directly linked to the health and well-being of successful executives, owing to their ability to provide freedom from hassles. Add to this list of perks the freedom to set one's own schedule, address tasks of interest, and "escape" to private enclaves such as Palm Springs, and you begin to see the major impact that success can have upon an individual's happiness and pleasure.

## PSYCHOLOGICAL CONTROL OR POWER

Psychologists and businessmen alike typically define control as a state of mind or mental attitude that enables an individual to determine the course of events before him. Having a sense of "self-efficacy" and being an "origin" rather than a "pawn" are two of the ways in which psychologists have tried to encapsulate the essence of this attribute. For businessmen, having a "take charge" attitude would seem to capture the meaning.

Regardless of which exact defintion of the term you prefer, a healthy sense of control is extremely favorable from a psychological perspective. Yet for many Americans, the term "control" is inextricably linked to notions of "power," which may conjure up a series of very negative associations. Power, control's sibling, is typically used to refer to states of influence over others—legitimate or otherwise. As one of the positive consequences of success, control is most accurately understood to represent an influence over one's personal surroundings and internal states rather than influence over other people. Hence, autonomy might be a synonym. A sense of personal mastery might be another.

The distinction between control and power is most useful when power is used to imply the *unauthorized* imposition of one's will upon a situation or a person. Success can give rise to power of this sort, but the exercise of one's capacity to dominate usually does not give rise to feelings of authentic pleasure. Instead, domination, or for that matter control that enables an individual to forcibly impose his will on those who are less powerful, represents a psychologically disordered state that to most people is not gratifying in the way that personal mastery or self-control born of success can be.

When we conceive of power in America today, the name Armand Hammer springs to mind. The octogenarian chairman of Occidental Petroleum Corporation is the beneficiary of what *Newsweek* calls "the ultimate executive perk: he gets to operate an entire $19 billion company as if it were his private fiefdom."[15] Hammer's exercise of power typically evokes divided opinions. Although credited with building Occidental Petroleum from what was a tiny oil-production company in 1957 into the giant it is today, Hammer is also accused of being responsible for bloodletting within the corporation's executive ranks.[16] Exercising his power to determine the fate of other corporate officers earned him a reputation for firing presidents at an unprecedented rate—six in 16 years as chairman.[17]

One example of the healthy exercise of power or control can be found among successful executives who prefer to exert their influence over fiefdoms that are truly personal. Many have created miniuniverses totally of their making. William McGowan, who owns 50% of MCI Communications, recently purchased a home in Washington D.C.'s Georgetown district and converted it into a private playland: "Pushbuttons control all manner of gadgets; lighting panels on every floor, a laser-disk stereo system that can be turned on by infrared signals from any room. And in the back patio, a Jacuzzi whirlpool bath stands surrounded by fake boulders."[18]

Mr. and Mrs. Robert J. Dole were christened "America's Power Couple" in 1983. At the time *Newsweek* described the Doles' qualification for such a prestigious accolade, Mr. Dole was the senior senator from Kansas and chairman of the Senate Finance Committee. *Newsweek* described his committee as "powerful" and went on to note that "his legislative domain extends over taxes, social security, Medicaid and other programs that affect the lives of all Americans." (He later went on to the more powerful post of Senate Majority Leader.) Mrs. Dole, Secretary of Transportation, had her power described as follows: "she oversees 62,500 employees and a $27 billion budget and is the first woman ever to head a branch of the U.S. armed forces—the Coast Guard."[19]

When you distill the descriptions of power listed above down to their essentials, it becomes clear that this derivative of success brings about happiness and pleasure by providing an opportunity to exert control over valued resources: corporations, private fantasy lands, or programs that affect the lives of all Americans. Dr. David Kipnis, a psychologist who has made extensive studies of people who exercise power, explored the psychological basis for deriving a sense of pleasure and happiness from the power of success. "Every study indicates that mental health and self-satisfaction are connected with position," said Kipnis.[20] He went on to note: "The more resources you control, the better you feel."

Other mental health professionals agree. Psychiatrist Dr. Bertram S. Brown claimed, after years of treating people who held power in Washington, D.C., "exercising power is the most effective short-range antidepressant in the world."[21] Power can even improve the sex life of the successful. According to Henry Kissinger, one of the most noted power brokers in recent times, "Power is the ultimate aphrodisiac."[22]

The satisfaction afforded by control and power is universally appealing. While some success-seekers may honestly wish never to bask in the glory of fame, most men and women long for the pleasure provided by power. We all want to control our personal fiefdoms. Archie Bunker bellowed about the chronic slights he suffered in the "outside world," but had his need for power satisfied by controlling access to his personal chair. Armand Hammer's "chair" atop the board of Occidental Petroleum is infinitely more consequential, but at a functional level, both he and Archie exercise the same type of power. Whether our rule extends over a living room or a corporation, the motivation is the same: we seek, at some fundamental level, to deny the uncertainty of life and the vulnerability we all experience, by obtaining and exercising power.

Power is one means of attacking head on the uglier side of life despite the fact that you'll never defeat it. Those who have power feel better, because by controlling their world, they can exclude many of the reminders of vulnerability and uncertainty that would otherwise plague them. Controlling resources imposes a *predictability* on the world and blots out reminders that some day one's well-being may be threatened. In a similar vein, holding power over the fates of others is thrilling since it suggests that one can, like a divine force, control a person's destiny. Whereas in the case of corporation chairmen it may begin with the fates of subordinates whom they can hire, promote, or fire, the real wish of those exercising power is ultimately to exert absolute and final control over their own destiny.

Success and its concomitant power will permit an individual to exert a greater degree of control over his fate than that available to an individual who is not distinguished in any way. The danger in this reasoned conclusion comes from assuming that power and/or money will lead to a fountain of youth or the mechanism needed to turn back the hands of time. Those successful people who know the limitations of their power are destined to enjoy the benefits derived from its full exercise for a long time. Those who don't are doomed to suffer severe disappointment.

Following Kissinger's assertion that power is the ultimate aphrodisiac, we can assume that it has a seductive appeal as well. Similarly, the pleasure derived from the prestige of success or the freedoms derived from success can blind an individual to the burdens imposed by riches and fame. The next chapter examines the attitudes and circumstances necessary to derive a full measure of satisfaction from success. Without the prerequisite capacity to accept and enjoy success, many people become almost "drunk" on the benefits it provides and ignore the way in which the positive consequences of success can also give rise to The Success Syndrome.

Chapter Four

# HOW TO FEEL SUCCESSFUL

*A man who has been the indisputable favorite of his mother keeps for life the feeling of a conqueror, that confidence of success that often induces real success.*

Sigmund Freud

As a consultant to executives stressed by success, I have learned more and more about why certain individuals succeed in business. Though this book is not written as a "how-to" manual for success-seekers, this chapter will recount the fundamental lessons I learned regarding the acquisition of success. The goal of this exercise will be to identify why some people can and do accept success when it becomes available and why others, who fall victim to The Success Syndrome, cannot.

At one time or another, virtually all of my executive patients account for their success in terms reminiscent of the "success = 10% inspiration and 90% perspiration" formula, so overused in motivational seminars and locker rooms. They typically offer this very superficial explanation at the initiation of therapy, before much self-inspection takes place. Once they are comfortable enough to examine themselves more critically, each "stressed-by-success" business executive eventually points to one aspect of his personality, such as leadership ability, interpersonal skills, self-discipline, or brains, in attempting to account for his prominence.

Personal traits are the factors that the outside world

typically uses to explain the success of those who have "made it." Not surprisingly, traits relating to interpersonal skills are the ones most commonly cited as being responsible for making or breaking an individual possessed of God-given talents. For example, *Time Magazine* indicated that their 1985 Man of the Year, entrepreneur, Olympic organizer, and Major League Baseball Commissioner Peter Ueberroth, is a superb social strategist. In particular, he was cited for his skill in the use of strategic *downward* self-promotion (described earlier), by which he can disarm any opposition: "Over the years he has perfected a calculating public modesty, down-playing himself about, say, his mediocre college grades. But behind the self-deprecation is a huge ego and a steely inner toughness. . . . He is a creative energizer of people . . . a natural teacher and leader."[1]

Invoking supersalesman and multimillionaire CEO Lee Iacocca again, we should note his endorsement of the notion that interpersonal skills determine which capable individuals will cut through the pack to succeed, and which will be left behind with mere potential. According to Iacocca, the key to management and success in business is the ability to "handle" people: "I've seen a lot of guys who are smarter than I am and a lot who know more about cars. And yet I've lost them in the smoke. Why? Because I'm tough? No. You don't succeed for very long by kicking people around. You've got to know how to talk to them, plain and simple."[2]

Yet assume that an individual with ability and energy is not cursed with a character flaw that alienates people. Is it safe to assume that with his raw talent and an intensive study of Dale Carnegie's *How to Win Friends and Influence People* he'll succeed? Unfortunately, no. Virtually every patient I have treated, before his psychotherapy ended, acknowledged a "bottom-line" causal agent more responsible for his success than any endearing personal trait.

Each, with no false modesty or strategic downward self-promotion intended, told me that in order to be successful you had to be *lucky!*

This opinion is echoed widely by the businessmen I consult for as well as by observers of prominent people. In recently featured cover stories describing the career development of two prominent professionals, *The New York Times Magazine* stressed the role of luck, good fortune, and fate in their climb to the top. Molecular biologist John Baxter, a leading force in the field of recombinant DNA technology and a strong contender for a Nobel Prize, is said to have had his career shaped and blessed by the fortuitous intervention of an eminent molecular biologist who assumed the role of mentor in his professional life. As the *Times* notes: "In science, as in other human endeavors, brilliance and ambition and determination are not enough. Ultimate success often depends on the tenuous personal bond that may develop between a young scientist and someone older who can inspire him and open doors."[3] And falling in with the right mentor is often a matter of luck.

Another case in point is that of the United States Attorney from New York, Rudolph W. Giuliani, who, in waging a successful war against organized crime, is being considered for much higher political office. Though he is unquestionably a tough and effective prosecutor, some observers attribute his prominence more to being in the right place at the right time than to mere ability. According to one report, the indictments against prominent organized crime figures being handled by Giuliani "are the result of a massive law-enforcement campaign that has taken 20 years" and Giuliani is in the position of being the lucky guy who gets to handle the cases now.[4]

Virtually every executive that I interviewed while conducting research on the stress of success indicated that his

career was shaped by some form of "luck" despite the fact
that some were reluctant to use that particular term in
accounting for their success. Synonyms such as "fortunate," "well-connected," "timely," and "opportune" were
used. But no matter how they described the auspicious
circumstances that aligned to advance their business plans
and/or gambles, they all acknowledged that getting to the
top is impossible without cooperation from whatever forces
control or account for "the breaks."

Norman S. Rabb, an executive I have come to know
through my work but who is not a patient of mine, provided me with a sterling example of the role of luck in
precipitating business success. He is one of the three brothers whose partnership launched and developed STOP & SHOP
supermarkets into one of the ten largest grocery chains in
the United States.

At the age of 65, after 40 years with STOP & SHOP, Rabb
has retired from a role of active participation in the business, though he continues to remain a director for life. In
addition to having developed a successful and thriving
business, Rabb has been honored for a host of humanitarian efforts. He was a Founding Trustee of Brandeis University, and an Honorary Life Trustee of a number of phi-
lanthropic groups as well as a prominent hospital in Boston.
By every possible criterion or set of standards available,
Rabb is a success.

At a dinner party given several months after his retirement, Rabb had an opportunity to sample some chopped
liver served with an exotic form of toasted bread that he
had never seen before. A fan of chopped liver, Rabb sam-
pled again and again, and soon realized that he was growing fond of the unique bread. When he asked the hostess
to describe what the liver was being served on, he learned
that it was a Syrian bread, pita bread, actually sold in his

STOP & SHOP stores and produced primarily by a local woman working out of her small family bakery.

What transpired after this party is a classic success story. Rabb followed up his enthusiasm for this little-known bread with calls to STOP & SHOP's bakery manager to learn more about the product. Next came a call to the woman who was the chief supplier of the bread. As Rabb tells the story, the woman, who was then working 14 hours a day to bake and distribute her bread, told him that she had been praying to St. Anthony for a savior to provide her with the merchandising skills necessary to remain in business. Upon meeting Rabb she claimed he was the man St. Anthony sent. He was.

The marriage of Rabb's marketing brilliance and this woman's product sired the Sahara Bread Corporation, which grew from a tiny business with no national recognition into a business with sales totaling several million dollars a year. In 1980, when Rabb sold this business to the Thomas' English Muffin division of Corn Products Refining Company International, he realized a handsome profit on the investment he had made in a little-known foreign bread.

Although the lion's share of the credit for creating the huge success realized by the Sahara Bread Corporation goes to Rabb, it is undeniably true that, were it not for the quality product he was merchandising, it would never have sold as well as it did. Credit for this component of the Sahara Bread Corporation rests solely in the hands of the woman who baked the bread Rabb sold to the nation. Considering the magnitude of her contribution to Rabb's success, it is fitting that she was comparably rewarded. According to Rabb, the woman served as a consultant for CPC International for two years after the sale of Sahara Bread. For this work and the sale of her business, she purportedly received "a fortune."

While Syrian bread or the "pita pocket" will probably never replace the hamburger or hot dog roll as the bread-stuff of America, it has been embraced by all segments of society. Why? Largely because a businessman with marketing strengths enjoyed chopped liver and was lucky enough to attend a party where it was served with a bread that was pleasing to his palate. As Rabb put it, "If they had served chopped herring instead, there would never have been a Sahara Bread Corporation."

## SELF-ESTEEM: THE LINK BETWEEN ABILITY AND SUCCESS

Was Norman Rabb's success story with Sahara Bread really just a matter of luck? Hardly. He was extremely fortunate that the hors d'oeuvres at one particularly fateful party were to his liking, and that he was exposed to a golden opportunity: a relatively unknown and undermarketed product with the potential for mass appeal. He was also lucky to have found an incredibly hard-working business partner who produced a quality product that he could market with confidence. Yet only a combination of his insights, knowledge of the supermarket business, skills as a merchandiser, and hard work enabled Rabb to turn a good idea into a success. And he had one other attribute mandatory for the effective functioning of a man with vision. He had the *positive self-esteem* necessary to believe that his insight would be translatable into a product line that would turn a profit.

Thousands of people are exposed to golden opportunities in their lifetime, but only a handful capitalize on them. The next Pet Rock exists, albeit as yet unpackaged. Many people will notice it before the soon-to-be millionaire who recognizes it *and* markets it makes a killing. Why will

one entrepreneur with vision succeed in bringing to frui-
tion a product that others "see" but fail to capitalize on?
Greater intelligence or foresight? Not really. There are
hundreds of smart paupers. The real reason is that most
people lack the gut feelings of self-confidence necessary
to muster the 90% perspiration needed to translate their
inspiration into a success.

Freud's insight into the origins of the "confidence of
success that often induces real success" was, not surprisingly, fairly accurate. A man (or woman) who has been
the indisputable favorite of his mother does have a greater
likelihood of developing the feelings necessary to become
a conqueror than the individual deprived of maternal affection. But while positive self-esteem cannot develop in
the absence of a significant amount of love, emotional support alone is never enough to provide an individual with
a truly solid sense of self-worth.

Positive self-esteem results from a personal recognition that one is loved *and competent*. Competence, simply
stated, refers to a capacity to deal effectively with the various demands of day-to-day living. It refers to an individual's capacity to respond to challenges successfully. Above
all else, competence is a feeling derived from *actually behaving* in a skilled manner so as to bring about an intended
outcome. The competent person feels "I can!"

In childhood, when a person's self-esteem is initially
developed, feelings of competence will derive from any
task involving mastery over some aspect of the environment or within oneself: successful toilet training and learning to identify objects in the world by their names are two
potential sources of competence. When a child successfully
executes tasks such as these *and* receives adult approval
for having done so, a positive sense of self-esteem should
develop. Thus, two component feelings are required for
the formation of a favorable self-concept: a sense of pleas-

ure and pride in "being" someone—derived from parental approval, and a sense of success and competence in "doing" something—derived from mastering a behavioral task.[5]

Mental health professionals have long been aware of the emotional problems and low self-esteem that result from an upbringing that provides love but no opportunities to develop a sense of competence. Some even maintain that it is impossible to have high self-esteem without significant levels of manifest proficiency in some skill or behavioral domain. Stories of "poor little rich girls" who languish in depressions brought about by their being given everything their hearts could desire, but never experiencing the joys that their friends feel in *making* toys and games, are common. Yet if a child is receiving love and can develop a sense of competence from tasks as basic as naming objects, why are individuals with robust, positive self-images so rare?

The definition of success developed earlier emphasized the fact that feelings of competence or ability could *not* develop unless an individual compares his performance against peers of equal rank, or rigorous performance standards. For a 10-year-old to feel "fast," he or she must win a race against competitors aged 10 or older. In the absence of appropriate competitors, ability can be evaluated in terms of surpassing some universally accepted standard: lifting more barbell weight than anyone in your age and weight bracket is one such example. The critical feature in both evaluative situations is that the performance criteria are *stable* and *clear-cut*. The determination of who is faster or stronger, and thus the winner, is independent of any evaluator's idiosyncratic opinion or judgment of ability.

The competence component of self-esteem must develop in an identical fashion. A person can only develop a favorable sense of self-regard in a context where there are well-defined and mutually agreed-upon expectations for what a "good performance" is. If an individual then acts in a manner that meets the criteria for a "good performance," and this intentional behavior is received with approval, a sense of positive self-esteem will emerge. Why then would self-esteem fail to develop in an individual who can perform competently? This would occur because his relative success or failure is linked to the judgments of another person.

In most instances where a lack of self-esteem exists *despite* a person's capacity to perform competently, that individual has been exposed to inconsistent or nonexistent performance criteria. Often this has occurred in childhood when parents shift their performance criteria depending on their mood. When "banging on drums for hours" is interpreted as "musical genius" on one day and "unruly behavior" on another, the would-be drummer finds it difficult to know how to act. Multiply this inconsistency by several years, and it is easy to see how some highly competent children learn to perform well *without* developing a positive self-regard.

Another scenario that can account for a failure to instill talented children with a sense of positive self-regard occurs when the criteria for success or failure are inextricably linked to parents' personal judgments. Although it is unquestionably imperative that a young child frequently hear that he or she is "mommy's sweetheart," a certain danger exists if the child never does anything to deserve such praise. If a child is praised independent of his competent performances and cannot determine why he has received approval, he is rendered incapable of providing self-generated approval in the absence of mommy's accolades.

If mommy is absent for extended periods, the child will be totally deprived of the supportive feedback he has come to depend on. Alternatively, if praise is linked to performance, a reexecution of previously praised behaviors can be reinforcing in much the same manner as mommy's praise. By accomplishing a performance that previously elicited desired feedback from loved ones, the child derives satisfaction not only from the realization that "I can do it," but from the *recollection* that those who matter most feel that "doing it" is very good.

The preceding argument should not be interpreted as advocating a parenting style that withholds love until a competent performance has been accomplished. On the contrary, periodic, unconditional positive regard is necessary for a healthy development. The key element here, however, is periodic. If praise is never linked with the mastery of a performance demand, it loses its significance and meaning because the question of "why" praise was delivered is left unanswered.

Returning to the question of how someone can be made to feel successful, we can now see that the answer is he can't. He can *earn* a sense of competence and develop, through a series of recognized achievements, a belief in his ability to master life's challenges. This will serve as the foundation for a sense of positive self-esteem if the recognition he receives is loving. But self-esteem and self-worth cannot be bestowed upon an individual through inheritance and birthright or even verbal assurances and encouragements. Hence, being the indisputable favorite of one's mother will not give a child "the feeling of a conqueror" as Freud maintained, unless the would-be conqueror periodically accomplishes tasks deserving of "favorite son" status.

## EXECUTIVE SELF-ESTEEM

The principle of needing to master tasks defined in terms of clear-cut expectations as a prerequisite to deriving a positive sense of self-esteem is as relevant to the adult psyche as it is to the developing child's. Several currently popular how-to manuals for executives patterned after *The One Minute Manager*[6] develop this fundamental principle of behavioral psychology into the cornerstone of modern personnel management theory. Basically, the formula boils down to the following: Define a goal explicitly, and then deliver positive or negative feedback to an employee in terms of his performance *on that task alone. Do not give feedback that is personal* such as "poor worker" or "good employee." Make feedback task-based (e.g., "excellent report"), and then follow it with rewards (raises, promotions) as a means of building an employee's self-esteem.

The issue left unaddressed by most of today's executive how-to primers is what it takes to deliver *One Minute*-type feedback to employees. Few studies of the executive ego emphasize the critical link between effective management styles and a strong sense of positive self-esteem. While a great many CEOs can manage with terror tactics and brute force, occasionally getting the job done well, such productivity is often obtained at the expense of valuable employees who resign rather than risk their psychic stability. Truly effective managers, who lead via strength of character—who keep valuable employees as well as turn out products—have the feeling of the conqueror described by Freud. As we now know, these executives have been nurtured, and have simultaneously developed a strong sense of competence.

Professor Jay W. Lorsch of Harvard Business School has commented upon the psychological makeup necessary for creative decision-making in business: "The common image is that business decision-making is very logical and very rational. But we have found that the process is more intuitive and judgmental and experience-based than most people think. We found that what sets the successful chief executive officer apart is that he has a strong sense of vision

and he really drives the organization toward that vision."[7]
Like someone who tastes an exotic bread, likes it, and,
because he knows what it takes to sell it to the nation, can
turn a one-woman bakery into a million dollar enterprise.

The executive who translates a thought into a vision
and then into a success, like Freud's conqueror, has the
confidence of success that can induce real success. He has
mastered numerous tasks and requirements en route to
the top, and has received approval for doing so. A stable
sense of positive self-esteem is derived from actions that
inform a person *why* he has achieved and, by extension,
*how* he can achieve again and again. Being loved just for
who you are is something that must be present to enable
infants to start their lives with a sense of fundamental
*security*. A sense of competence can only develop when
this sense of well-being is supplemented by evidence of
the ability to master a range of challenges.

There is an Oriental proverb that states, essentially,
"If you give a hungry man a fish you can keep him alive.
If you *teach* a hungry man to fish, you give him a livelihood." The learning experience is clearly preferable for the
hungry man's self-esteem. Learning to fish is also the only
way in which this man will ever be able to *feel* successful.
As Professor Lorsch noted, the individual who will succeed in developing a business idea into a successful product has an *experiential* base upon which to draw. In short,
he has some history of making things work and, as a result,
has a sense of positive self-esteem.

The notion that success derives from "10% inspiration
and 90% perspiration" is not supported by the anecdotal
reports of successful business executives. According to those
with a track record of succeeding, a number of other factors

determine who will get to the top of the heap. When gross differences in ability are controlled for, I have seen time and time again that personality traits such as social skills and interpersonal ease are central determinants of success in the business world. More important, still, are luck, good connections, timing, and the like. Successful people from all walks of life acknowledge that without the proper breaks, no amount of ability or charm can bring about success.

Yet the most crucial key to opening doors that are made accessible through good fortune is a sense of positive self-esteem. The person who can capitalize on those opportunities that knock once or several times is the one who has an inner sense of confidence in his competence to convert possibilities into successful products. Because of the high regard he has experienced in the past, the person with positive self-esteem has the psychological energy to doggedly pursue his goals despite impediments, frustrations, and other limitations.

Self-esteem cannot be given or "awarded" by others. Love in the absence of feelings of competency fails to foster positive self-esteem. In the chapters that follow, I will examine how praise, presented independent of praiseworthy performance, can do more damage than merely thwart the process of building a favorable self-conception. Specifically, our attention can now turn to the many ways in which the pressures and false promise inherent in verbal rewards devoid of an experiential base cause many of the negative outcomes of The Success Syndrome.

Part Two

# THE SUCCESS SYNDROME: EXPECTATIONS, OBLIGATIONS, AND STRESS

## Chapter Five

# THE STRESS OF SUCCESS

*I feel lousy about my celebrity. Lousy.*
*Now I have to share my life with everybody.*
Lee Iacocca (from an interview in 1986)


*Success is like some horrible disaster*
*Worse than your house burning*
Malcolm Lowry

The demand to perform is the root cause of psychological stress. Stress develops when an individual is obligated or forced to fulfill a requirement, solve a problem, or adapt to a change in his environment *that exceeds his capacity to perform*. More specifically, the process of struggling in vain to respond to a performance demand may result in an individual's suffering acute or chronic disorders, ranging in severity from headaches to ulcers to coronary heart disease.[1]

The requirement to drive a car a distance of 10 miles on a particular road will likely generate little or no stress for any licensed driver en route to his favorite bakery. Obtaining fresh croissants is typically a low-threat performance demand. This same route would be deemed a potential stressor if an individual were traveling from home to work on a crowded highway. Were he due at work at 8:30 and found that he was in the midst of heavy traffic at 9:15, he would experience considerable stress. If this were the fifth such occurrence in a month and he had already been warned that tardiness was jeopardizing his future with the corporation, this trip would generate even greater stress. As the importance of any outcome (getting between points A and B) increases, the threat posed by a failure to perform the required task becomes greater. In turn, greater levels of threat generate correspondingly greater levels of stress.

This type of negative stress—technically called *distress*—is psychologically and physically debilitating. Commuters who are constantly subjected to traffic jams are prone to develop ulcers, headaches, and hypertension *if* these standstills are threatening their job security, peace of mind, or well-being in any way. There is another type of stress, however, called *eustress*, which is beneficial to one's health and equanimity. Eustress derives from a demand to perform on levels equal to or only slightly exceeding past performances. Performance demands that give rise to the experience of eustress do not exceed one's expected or anticipated performance capabilities. Referred to in both professional and common parlance as *challenges*, they typically evoke a feeling of exhilaration.

The challenge of an "expert" slope to the well-seasoned "advanced intermediate" skier is an example of the type of situation that could generate eustress. Even if this skier had never before negotiated a slope of this degree of difficulty, were he to view it as within his range of probable performance capabilities, he would feel little or no threat in "taking it on." Most important, the successful execution of this challenge would provide him with abundant feelings of joy and excitement. Another example of such exhilaration would be that experienced by an individual promoted to a position he was psychologically prepared to assume.

The sole determinant of whether the demand to perform will cause distress or eustress rests upon an individual's perception of that demand. When a demand creates a challenge replete with the excitement of anticipated conquests, an individual will experience eustress. When a demand threatens his sense of well-being, feelings of distress will overcome him. This is commonly referred to as stress.

Thus, any performance requirement is capable of generating *either* stress or eustress depending upon what goes on within "the eye of the beholder." A variety of life experiences deemed "exciting" or "challenging" to a vast majority of individuals (e.g., promotions, victories) may pose threats to others because of their psychological makeup and/or readiness to assume challenges. In the chapters that follow, we will examine in detail the various psychological factors that determine if people who assume new roles view the world as dominated by either challenges or threats. For the moment it is important to recognize that, for certain people, any circumstance that conveys a demand to perform may generate feelings of stress and precipitate stress-related disease.

Malcolm Lowry showed a great deal of psychological sensitivity in selecting the burning of one's house as an example of a disaster and a metaphor for success. In point of fact, both are inordinately stressful life experiences. At a behavioral level, house fires force people to cope with performing in many new and difficult ways. The aftermath of the burning of your house forces you to seek all the necessities of life—food, clothing, shelter—while simultaneously attending to newfound legal and financial problems. When your home is destroyed, you are separated from your community and friends at the very moment you need them most. Moreover, victims of fires find themselves dependent on a variety of strangers for assistance, be they firefighters or insurance agents. How does the stress of success compare with this?

Actually, they are very similar. Becoming successful forces an individual to confront and cope with countless new and difficult performance demands in exactly the same way as the loss of a home would. To cope with the consequences of success, an individual would be required to change his living habits, adjust his interpersonal relationships, and, most important, adjust his personal standards for the behaviors he will expect of *himself*. In fact, every aspect of his life would be subjected to increased performance demands—and their by-product, stress. Examining the way in which success has forced some successful people to cope with increased levels of stress will help clarify this point.

## THE NEED TO RESTRUCTURE YOUR WORLD AS A CONSEQUENCE OF SUCCESS

Earlier we explored the way in which success can reduce stress by providing resources that eliminate daily hassles. Having secretaries, assistants, private cars, dining rooms, and the like makes transactions in the workworld more tolerable and less time-consuming. Perks have even been linked to the superior health and life expectancy enjoyed by successful executives.[2] Yet as we will see repeatedly in the pages that follow, the consequences of success can create a "down" side as well.

When a person's success lifts him from the ranks of the well-to-do to levels of stardom, insulation from daily activities is no longer a benefit or perk; it becomes a necessity. If your corporation earns record profits, it is truly gratifying to be able to reward yourself with a chauffeured limousine. However, if your profits derive from making solid-gold or platinum records, a chauffeured limousine takes on a different meaning. No longer is it merely a relaxing or luxurious mode of transportation. It is now a life-protection system, most probably bulletproofed to separate "a star" from crazed fans. For the successful artist or star from any given field, achieving a huge success paradoxically deprives him of the opportunity to enjoy certain fruits of his labors.

Larry Bird, the superstar basketball player who has won more than his share of the sport's achievement awards since joining the NBA, describes himself in terms that make him sound like a victim of success. This simple man, affectionately nicknamed the "Hick from French Lick" (Indiana, his hometown), has not reveled in the fruits of success as one would suspect he could. This legendary athlete, who earns in excess of $2 million a year, has noted, "I like being [financially] secure, but it's strange when you have all this money but you can't go into a mall and spend it."[3]

Why is it that a man who is 6'10" tall, perfectly coordinated, and worth millions cannot go shopping? Quite simply, he would be harassed by autograph-seeking, albeit well-intentioned, fans who would literally drive him crazy. Here is a case where stature—both in size and in name—cannot protect a successful person from hassles. Not that Bird is really subjected to the type of daily hassles that were linked to stress-related disorders by a group of Stanford University researchers. On the contrary, successful people, particularly the supersuccessful, are subjected to a unique brand of hassles that derive from attaining success. These "star hassles" might appear to be quite glamorous when compared to the average person's irritants (e.g., the annoyance of paparazzi versus the frustration of waiting for the train), but the impact on the successful person's body and psyche takes its toll. The stress they cause is real.

Most of the hassles that successful people suffer are directly attributable to the fact that many of them attain celebrity status. To hear celebrities tell it, acquiring "a name" is not a uniformly positive experience. The lament of Lee Iacocca, which opened this chapter, is a perfect case in point. In response to a press question about his personal life, tennis star John McEnroe asserted: "Being a celebrity like I am is like being raped. You can't do anything about it."[4] Geraldine Ferraro, the former Congresswoman from Queens, New York, who became the first female vice-presidential candidate on a major party's national ticket, suffered inordinate stress as a result of her extraordinary accomplishment and subsequent campaigning for public office. While on the campaign trail, she was so distressed that questions of her mental stability arose:

> The tension was beginning to get to me. I started to bite my nails, a habit I'd gotten over as a kid. And to eat. I'd always been able to leave a meal with food still on the plate. Now I started to eat almost compulsively—gaining thirteen pounds by the end of the campaign. I had never thought of myself as a neurotic person, but it was hard for me to decide whether I was developing a persecution complex or whether, indeed, I was being persecuted.[5]

By the end of the campaign, although relieved to be through with what at times had been an ordeal, Ferraro was not entirely able to free herself from the hassles that will undoubtedly remain with her for a long time to come:

> In the last days of the campaign, the historical significance of my candidacy became more apparent to me. Whether we won or lost, I would still go down on the books as the first woman vice-presidential candidate of a major party, an extraordinary fact that I often overlooked in the heat of the campaign.
> . . . on Election Day [I felt] . . . relief that the campaign was all over. But there was still craziness out there. When we came out of church, a reporter fired dumb questions at me . . . "Were you praying for an upset victory?" What I wanted to say was that I was thanking God I wouldn't have to face people like him again for a while. . . .[6]

In attempting to avoid the hassles derived from celebrity status, a successful person who is evasive or uses his resources to seclude himself from the public may be seen as being an aloof or arrogant personality. Instead, they should be seen as engaging in fundamental coping strategies enacted in response to substantial levels of stress. More to the point, we can see that they are being forced to make major adjustments in their life in order to cope with performance demands derived from success. Bodyguards, security fences, press agents, and secret hideaways may appear glamorous to outsiders looking in. To those successful people who *need* them, however, they are health aids on a par with crutches, wheelchairs, and oxygen tents. How many of us envy invalids?

## STRAINS AND BREAKDOWNS WITHIN INTERPERSONAL RELATIONSHIPS CAUSED BY SUCCESS

Who, in their right mind, would *not* want to win a lottery? How could prizes in excess of $1 million a year for 20 years be bad? Could these fantastic winnings precipitate stress? Yes, and for a significant number of people they do.

Although winning a lottery does not make someone *truly* successful, it does make him instantly rich, thereby providing some of the luxuries and imposing many of the burdens assumed by the more "legitimately" successful. Anecdotal reports documenting the trials and tribulations of lottery winners attest to the fact that instant riches can threaten friendships, and put a strain on all interpersonal and intrafamilial relationships. According to one lottery winner: "We got to know who our real friends are. They are the ones who didn't have their hands out."[7]

This distressed lottery winner was subjected to unique and undesirable performance demands because of his instant riches: he was expected to behave more generously and supportively than he had prior to acquiring wealth. Although virtually any lottery winner can cope with this performance demand (since any increase in giving would fulfill the requirements of becoming *more* generous), he may legitimately question "Why should I?" More to the point, the threat inherent in the demand to behave more generously lies in the potential loss of love linked to not giving in the "appropriate" manner. Beyond questioning why he should spread his new wealth around, he who becomes instantly rich may come to wonder what and whom he will lose if he doesn't.

The dilemma of instant riches is definitely not restricted to lottery winners. In fact, those who benefit from lucky outcomes are often spared the burden of others' jealously, since those who have not been smiled upon by Lady Luck believe that someday they too can "score." The people who suffer the most from instant riches are the ones who *achieve* success. Many entrepreneurs, who "strike it rich" through a combination of foresight and incisive actions, find their business acumen "rewarded" by the devastation of interpersonal relationships. Their circumstance is doubly perilous since their good fortune is attributable to something that is not randomly distributed—intelligence.

Those who become instantly rich must walk a sky-high emotional tightrope with both friends and family members. On the one hand, their new status threatens existing relationships if they are not generous and forthcoming. On the other hand, the appropriate level of giving is difficult to achieve even for those desirous of spreading the wealth. Frequently, someone can give too much, appearing to be a patsy undeserving of respect. It is also often the case that "overgiving" smacks of arrogance and braggadocio, which can be more offensive than niggardliness. Is there a resolution to this dilemma? Probably not, and this is one of the many reasons why success is often stressful. If we recall that stress is an emotional derivative of performance demands that exceed an individual's capabilities, we can see how the suddenly rich become stressed trying to navigate an uncharted course between others' judgments of greediness or grandiosity. Since it is impossible to adopt an attitude toward money that will please everyone, only two possibilities exist. Either ignore the wishes of others and handle your wealth as you see fit—handing it out or holding on to it—or subject yourself to a lifetime of continual readjustments to varying performance demands—the primary cause of stress.

## HOW SUCCESS STRESSES LOVE

Making money, achieving fame, and having power open most of the doors on earth worth opening. That is, except those to purely *personal* relationships. One of the reasons why successful people, particularly media personalities and those from aristocratic backgrounds, are both socially and sexually inbred with such consistency, is the need to avoid the stress of inequitable relationships. When couples are comprised of one individual from a successful background and one who is not, significant interpersonal problems are almost inevitable.

A potentially disruptive consequence of inequitable relationships (i.e., one rich, one not) is that *both* parties are cognizant of the possibility that the less successful of the two has a salient reason apart from affection for sustaining the involvement. The success (money, fame) of the one who has it can, in and of itself, account for why a person without comparable resources might sustain a relationship. This is not to imply that every average person who marries "up" is a gold digger. It is apparent to all interested parties, however, that marrying "money" does have its advantages.

For the individual with the money or other trappings of success, marrying someone without comparable resources can precipitate troublesome doubts. As psychological research demonstrates, when more than one plausible cause exists for a particular outcome (e.g., marriage), there is much less certainty as to why the event took place than if only one plausible cause existed.[8] The successful party always harbors some suspicion that were it not for the fact that he/she was successful, his/her lover would not have been quite as interested.

An even more potentially damaging fear is that the "unsuccessful" lover, in order to remain in good standing in the relationship, will acquiesce to the successful one's wishes or demands despite conflicting feelings. To readers involved in relationships already dominated by power struggles, this circumstance must sound like heaven. But to those in positions of prominence and power (as we will see in later chapters), the luxury of having an *honest* confidant is worth more than a boatload of gold.

## EXECUTIVES' SPOUSES

The "double-edged" quality of success cuts into the lives of "unsuccessful" spouses as deeply as it does into the lives of those who have achieved success. An individual "marrying money" typically finds that it is very difficult to engage in a normal social life aware that people question whether you are devoted to your mate or his/her millions. Looks can't kill, but they can cause inordinate emotional discomfort. They can also lead a person to question his own motives owing to the overwhelming weight of the evidence in favor of inferring a "mercenary" intent. Even on those occasions when a guilty verdict is not reached, the process of evaluating one's love for another on the basis of doubts raised by others can cause extreme psychological distress.

In the course of both studying and treating male executives, I have had numerous occasions to interview their wives. Through these interviews, I have been able to document an intriguing phenomenon unique to executives' wives who did *not* come from wealthy backgrounds prior to their marriage, and were not themselves successful. Each and every one of these women told me of fighting with, or pulling away from, her husband at some point in their relationship, fearing that his success (money, status) was controlling or determining her affection for him. Although the husband's success might have been part of his appeal at some point in time, each of these women reported at least one significant period in their relationship when it became a source of resentment. As one tearful wife told me in a quivering voice: "It's impossible not to love him the way he spoils me with gifts, trips, access to big names and great events . . . sometimes I feel I *have to* love him or my friends would think I'm crazy! I just wish I were free to *not* love him . . . if he were only not so wealthy but had his same personality, things would be great."

This woman's sentiments are not at all aberrant or reflective of personality flaws. Psychologists and philosophers alike have argued that one of the primary drives experienced by humans is the drive to be free. As this executive's wife demonstrated in poignant terms, the drive to be free extends to the freedom to love without the pressures imposed by a spouse's wealth. The motivation or drive to be free is so strong that a person will actively contradict directives or demands that threaten his or her fundamental freedoms. In numerous laboratory studies, psychologists have observed that people who feel that their freedoms are threatened will engage in behaviors to demonstrate those very freedoms.[9]

Although the dominance and power of success can assume a cloak of subtlety—a presence more than a force—these qualities often threaten the freedom of expression of others. The story of "the emperor's new clothes" demonstrates that. Yet the townsfolk who saw the naked emperor had it easy; they didn't care if he wanted to believe he was the image of sartorial splendor. You can easily turn your back on someone who doesn't matter to you as a person. The problem for executives' spouses and other intimates of successful people is that they feel compelled to speak their true feelings. Yet to discern how they truly feel is extraordinarily difficult with the distracting dazzle of success clouding their thoughts. The resulting confusion is not only painful, it's stressful.

## THE EVIL EYE

Interpersonal difficulties are also common in friendships when one party is successful and the other is not, particularly if the relationship was initiated before the former became successful. Successful people commonly lament that they have lost friends as a result of their success. Every one of my patients whose psychological disorder is a consequence of success reports that soon after having attained his most cherished goals, someone from "the old neighborhood" asserted that he had either changed for the worse or had been "corrupted" by success and its trappings. These perceived changes were then offered as the reason why they avoided their old pal who, in the wake of his success, moved "uptown." In point of fact, those left behind are usually trying in vain to hide the bitterness and pain of envy.

This phenomenon should surprise no one familiar with the Bible, where jealousy and envy are frequent themes. Cain, a poor farmer, envied his brother Abel's success, and killed him. Joseph, the favorite son who wore a coat of many colors given to him by his father, was sold into slavery by jealous brothers.

In most cultures, including our own, people are often reluctant to disclose that they are successful owing to a fear that others will be envious—give them the evil eye—and bring harm to them. We hear of people who "knock wood" following compliments or disclosures of success (the noise from knocking will presumably distract the devils residing there who would punish those guilty of hubris). Similarly, "pleading poverty" is a common form of strategic self-presentation adopted by the highly successful wishing to protect themselves from jealous acquaintances.

An unfortunate corollary to this finding is that most of the successful people whom I have interviewed or treated report that the only type of new friendship they can form is with people of comparable status. It appears that successful people have difficulty forming trusting relationships with those they come in contact with because they fear that people may feign liking them in order to benefit from their power or influence. On countless occasions I've heard a highly successful patient lament, "I keep wondering if he likes me for who I am, or *what* I am?" If new acquaintances are on a "comparable footing," concerns regarding the basis of affection are unnecessary: If "what" they are is as important as "what" you are, you can trust that their friendly overtures do not belie manipulative intentions. Sadly, many successful people find that potentially rewarding relationships never get started because of the consequences of success.

Ironically, the most formidable performance demands successful people may ever have to face can emerge in interpersonal relationships. Because of the resources they control and the dominance they exercise over most social settings, successful people are faced with countless questions concerning the sincerity of those who call themselves friends. The emotional energy required to differentiate authentic friends from sycophants can generate considerable stress, but it is a "performance demand" most successful people attempt to meet. As we shall see below, the consequences of not knowing if acquaintances really care for you as a person or view you as a meal ticket are often psychologically devastating.

## THE STRESS DERIVED FROM CHANGING INTERNAL PERFORMANCE STANDARDS FOLLOWING SUCCESS

Every person reading this book once, in a time now long forgotten, took pride in his ability to tie his shoes. When Buster Browns and Keds were the "in" footwear, commanding ten stubby fingers to loop and knot two uncooperative strings was a major undertaking; completing the task successfully was a significant accomplishment. Now it seems ludicrous to think about the fact that Florsheims or Reeboks have laces that need to be tied. And just think of the *humiliation* we would experience if someone praised us for making a well-tied bow on our wing tips. Maturation and a history of mastering tasks turns yesterday's triumphs into today's trivialities.

Psychologists have studied the phenomenon of the shifting degrees of satisfaction that people derive from achievements over time. Their research has demonstrated that people almost always strive to perform at levels higher than prior performances. An individual's *level of aspiration* (LOA)—the standard by which a person evaluates his own performance—is also determined by what he would like to achieve on subsequent tasks given his age and proven ability.[10] Thus, although the grade-school athlete who wins the 100-yard dash will undoubtedly raise his LOA upon receipt of a blue ribbon, the psychologically healthy sprinter would forestall dreams of an Olympic Gold Medal until his or her legs have grown substantially. Aspirations of winning a high school varsity letter, while still somewhat excessive for a child in grade school, would be more appropriate than dreams of Olympic glory. This is not to say that accomplishments should not inspire dreams of greatness; they should. However, problems are likely to develop if dreams of greatness raise an individual's LOA to unattainable heights, given existing performance capabilities.

Successful people are often victims of their own LOAs escalating out of control. Although it is often the case that "nothing succeeds like success," when performances start approaching more rarefied levels of accomplishment, the adage "nothing *oppresses* like successes" may be more accurate.

According to the poet Robert Browning, "A man's reach should exceed his grasp, or what's a heaven for?" Although we may not get to heaven regardless of how consistently we raise our LOA, no one can deny that a moderate form of heaven-on-earth—eustress—is impossible without undertaking challenges that exceed our grasp. Many experiences of joy, thrills, and exhilaration would be impossible were it not for our innate drive to exceed past successes.

The paradox, however, lies in the fact that one's reach, which is guided by one's mind, may exceed one's physical capability to perform certain tasks. An unfortunate consequence of a string of successes is that both an individual's LOA as well as external performance demands will be raised to increased levels. The spiraling demands on performance that follow success must, at some point, exceed an individual's capabilities, since human abilities are finite whereas expectations are limitless. These ever-increasing performance demands ultimately come to be a source of constant stress.

The internal performance standards of a successful person may be affected by forces other than an innate tendency to elevate his LOA. One of the more devastating of these forces is that of *social* expectations. In simple terms, social expectations are the levels of aspiration that other, oftentimes related, people impose on the successful. Though similar to personal LOAs, social expectations are often insensitive to the limitations (physical or experiential) of the successful person. For this reason alone, they can be significantly more demanding or burdensome.[11]

Successful people who enter psychotherapy for "executive stress" almost always report being crippled by burdensome expectations. They complain that following most or all of their achievements, the people who matter most to them—parents, spouse, colleagues—convey either implicitly or explicitly their belief that still more can be accomplished. Regrettably, since these expectations are conveyed by those who are loved or admired, they have the force of reasonable performance demands. The pressure inherent in urgings such as "Come on son, you can still improve your fastball" or "If we capture just 2% more of the market we'll be ahead of XYZ Manufacturing" in the wake of success can generate debilitating levels of stress.

In my clinical practice, I find that those successful people who succumb to burdensome expectations look around after a significant accomplishment and ask, "Where do I go from here?" Instead of savoring deserved feelings of self-satisfaction, these individuals fall victim to the expectations of others. For individuals such as these, there is virtually no time to savor the joy of having met a challenge or attained a goal; new demands always loom on the horizon.

"Encore," "bravo," and "one more time" are accolades conveying appreciation of a performer's skills and talented performance. In addition to satisfying the performer, these cries are what psychologists call "reinforcing": they heighten the likelihood of having the performer repeat those praise-winning behaviors. In certain instances, however, praise, encouragement, and verbal rewards do not satisfy and reinforce performers. Instead, they too can create burdensome expectations and excessive performance demands. The successful person who incessantly has his reach exceed his grasp as he strives for heaven will probably suffer a stress-induced hell-on-earth until he is able to derive satisfaction from challenging, not threatening, levels of aspiration.

Consistent with the assertions of Malcolm Lowry, who likened success to the disaster of having one's house burn, we have seen that several consequences of success do, in fact, precipitate severe psychological stress. Once a person becomes successful, he must make painful adjustments in areas of his living arrangements, interpersonal relationships, and even his internal standards of acceptable behavior.

When the causes of stress are examined, we can see why success is a two-edged sword. Although moderate levels of success can enable individuals to cope more easily with daily hassles, the status of supersuccess can reverse this positive effect. Hence, successful people who become public figures are often imprisoned by their stardom rather than liberated by it. Similarly, the kind of popularity that is so coveted by most of us is denied those with great riches or fame. For the *crème de la crème*, success often breeds suspicion of others who lack their lofty status and tends to disrupt or preempt intimate relationships with individuals who might love them regardless of status and monetary differences. Finally, and most disturbing, whereas success can breed a boundless sense of self-worth, it can also impose performance expectations that are guaranteed to stress the most competent of individuals.

Making extensive adjustments in response to increased performance demands can severely stress an individual. When these adjustments are to one's self-conception, the results can be devastating. In the chapters to follow, we will examine in depth how being forced to readjust or change one's self-image in response to success can precipitate a wide range of psychological disorders.

Chapter Six

# HOW THE SUCCESSFUL BECOME VICTIMIZED

## Expectations and Praise

$$Self\text{-}esteem = \frac{Success}{Pretensions}$$

William James

We examined earlier how a person could feel successful. Differentiating the *acquisition* of success and its trappings from the *experience* of self-satisfaction and joy derived from reaching "the top" revealed that having it all does *not* necessarily mean enjoying it all. In order to enjoy success, a person must be led throughout his life to believe that he deserves favorable outcomes. In a word, the key to feeling successful is an entrenched sense of self-esteem.

Our understanding of The Success Syndrome is advanced significantly by examining philosopher/psychologist William James's insights into the relationship between self-esteem and success. His elegant formula presents, in exactly three words, what people have been searching to discover throughout recorded time: the way to increase positive self-esteem. Following James's formula, to enhance self-esteem you simply increase success or lower pretensions.

The problem here, quite obviously, is that "simply" increasing success is no simple matter. If achieving success were something that could be willed or attained by merely exerting effort, it would be far less consequential for those who achieve it. In fact, as described earlier, the skills and resources necessary to sustain a successful status are frequently quite complex. The pressures involved in living up to the expectations derived from success are one of the most, if not the most stressful consequences of success.

The trick, then, is to address pretensions. Not pretensions as commonly defined today—affectations, haughty displays, or presumptuous assertions—but as James intended. To understand James's definition of the term "pretensions," his formula should be rewritten as follows:

$$\text{Self-esteem} = \frac{\text{What has been accomplished}}{\text{What is possible or expected}}$$

Pretensions, as James used the term, are best understood as being *expectations* held about an individual's performance capabilities. The "relative" nature of success may now be seen to derive directly from the need to judge performances in context. For instance, the success of any particular performance outcome is determined directly by "who done it." As noted in an earlier chapter, tying one's shoes can be a significant source of self-esteem depending upon who you are. The degree of success represented by a given performance cannot be determined unless it can be compared to that expected by a member of an appropriate reference group. This reference group provides a normative standard that serves as a guideline for inferring *relative* merit.

Knotting laces is a successful act if accomplished by a victim of muscular dystrophy or a 2-year-old child. It is a competency expected *of* and *by* almost everyone over the age of 3. As noted in our previous discussion of expectations, they can derive from personally held beliefs as well as the opinions of others. Yet regardless of their origin, expectations have a tremendous influence over how people choose to behave as well as their feelings derived from the behavior and its consequences.

"To give up pretensions is as blessed a relief as to get them gratified," said William James in his writings on self-esteem.[1] Aspiring to achieve little or nothing relieves pressure and frees a person from worry. A supposedly satisfied Porgy (of Gershwin's *Porgy and Bess*) proclaimed, "I got plenty of nothin' and nothin's plenty for me."[2] With this attitude, he was virtually guaranteed a life devoid of disappointment and the stress derived from being bound to live up to performance requirements. Porgy climbed the ladder as far as *he* wished to go. Anyone whose primary goal is the avoidance of pain derived from failing is encouraged to adopt a "Porgy-like" renunciation of a lifestyle dedicated to achievement.

Yet everyone knows that Porgy, and many like him, renounce upward striving when they recognize that the path ahead of them is blocked or they lack sufficient resources to continue onward. Preemptive rejection—or "sour grapes" as Aesop called the strategy—is an easy way to avoid the hurt of not attaining goals we aspire to, but have little chance of reaching. Most people, not constrained as crippled Porgy was, continuously raise their level of aspiration throughout life. The danger in this otherwise perfectly healthy orientation toward achievement is that when higher goals are set, more burdensome expectations must be addressed.

## UNWANTED, UNFOUNDED, AND UNSHAKABLE EXPECTATIONS

One of the cruelest twists of fate associated with success is that many successful people are as trapped by their enviable circumstances as Porgy was by his handicap.

Whereas Porgy had to maintain that he was satisfied with a beggar's life because he lacked alternatives, rich and famous people often feel compelled to revel in a luxurious life-style or face social censure and ridicule. Adding insult to injury is the fact that if you are rich and famous you are deprived of an opportunity to declare that "nothin's plenty for me." Apart from those instances in which an individual renounces all aspects of a successful life-style in favor of one totally devoid of competitive aspirations or high-level expectations (e.g., Zen or monastic life-styles), it is difficult if not impossible to avoid the burden of expectations imposed by the status of being successful.

Another unfair and unfortunate aspect of this phenomenon is that the pressures of adhering to performance expectations and role requirements imposed upon successful people are often imposed upon their offspring as well. The net effect of these inappropriate performance expectations is often destructive to the mental health of successful people and their families.

The most salient example of this form of suffering can be found in stories about the Kennedys. This clan, arguably the most famous in the country, is the equivalent of American royalty. Unlike that of most royal families, however, the Kennedy mystique is based primarily on a history of success as opposed to mere genealogic succession. Only after amassing a fortune through shrewd business practices could the Kennedys parlay their wealth into a formidable political power base.

Yet few if any readers need to be updated on the trauma and suffering that has pervaded the lives of the children of, for example, the late Robert Kennedy. Despite, or possibly because of their money and what it has bought for them, these children and their cousins have had drug problems, in addition to emotional, career, and a variety of other painful and well-publicized difficulties.

Although a strong case could be made for ignoring the problems of the so-called "Kennedy children" since they are, in the aggregate, probably no more troubled than peers from other families, one has to wonder what role their "inherited success" has played in causing the problems so commonly reported by the media. Some insight into this question may be gained by examining a homily from St. Luke that Rose Kennedy reportedly quoted to her children and grandchildren at confirmations, graduations, and commencements: "To whom much is given, much will be required."[3] According to Peter Collier and David Horowitz, who have written about the Kennedys, this quote had special meaning for Bobby Kennedy. During the time following Jack's death, when Bobby was the functional head of the clan, he translated Rose's quote from St. Luke to mean, "America has been very good to the Kennedys. We all owe the country a debt of gratitude and public service."[4]

St. Luke's directive regarding the responsibilities of the wealthy—coupled with Bobby Kennedy's personal twist of this homily—convey inordinately burdensome expectations to a group of children who, having grown up in the midst of splendor, would have a hard time realizing that the way they lived wasn't "normal." Even if we assume that they recognized their privileged status and felt an authentic sense of gratitude for it, is it not oppressive to hear—at confirmations, graduations, and commencements as you are about to assume a more burdensome mantle of responsibility anyway—that you owe a *debt* to your nation because of your ancestry?

We should bear in mind that the "Kennedy children" were hearing this from the two heads of their clan, not a parish priest or school administrator. Although it is impossible to prove that Bobby's directives to his children regarding their debt to America caused their documented problems with drugs and school, it is reasonable to assume that his children labored throughout their life with greater performance expectations than most people could ever imagine. Thus, we might assume that for some of these children, the stress derived from burdensome expectations was too great for their young shoulders to bear.

Although it is always painful to learn that a young person has died from an overdose of drugs or alcohol, we feel it is all the more inappropriate when "he had so much going for him." When the press reported that the children of Art Linkletter, Louis Jourdan, and Paul Newman died as a result of involvement with drugs, people had to wonder: How, with all the power and influence of their successful fathers, could these children fail to be happy?

This very question, "how could they fail to be happy?," may be the *true* cause of death in the cases of many of the children of celebrities. The shadows cast by successful parents are often far too long to permit their offspring the room to develop identities of their own. This is not to say that a person's noble birthright will necessarily prove to be a hindrance. On the contrary, countless numbers of successful people, including Jack, Bobby, and Ted Kennedy, and the majority of their children, came from successful lineages that *facilitated* their own success. Yet in certain circumstances, for reasons that will be explored in greater detail in upcoming chapters, some children with successful parents are victimized by the pressures of having to live up to the family name.


## THE BOSS'S SON DILEMMA

Families with pedigrees comparable to the Kennedys are known to us owing to their enormous political power and wealth and the foundations they support. So it is not surprising that problems confronting a Getty, Rockefeller, or Carnegie find their way into print. Less well publicized is the fact that countless other families, successful enough to place silver spoons in the mouths of their offspring, can "doom" children to a lifetime of burdensome expectations as a result of the family's status within their community. In fact, depending upon the size of the community that one calls home, even moderate degrees of parental success have the potential to generate an imposing set of expectations for their "innocent" offspring.

At least 25% of my "executive stress" patients are the sons and daughters of prominent people in the Boston area. Suffering from what I call the "Boss's Son Dilemma," these children have had an upbringing in which "much has been given, and much is expected." That's the problem: they're aware of the blessings they have received as well as the burden of expectations they impose.

All of my "Boss's Son and Daughter" patients acknowledge that they have been given all "the breaks" that peers crave and quite frequently resent. Moreover, they are cognizant that their problems are a consequence of the fact that their parents' success (wealth, connections, and so on) does give them a "leg up" on the competition. With the advantages they have inherited at birth paving the way for them throughout their lives, anything they achieve appears to be less a function of their ability than would be the case were they "normal kids."

One severely depressed patient of mine, suffering from the Boss's Son Dilemma, lamented his pedigree in angry terms: "Sure my family name has been synonymous with [an industry] in this area for dozens of years, and it's true that I've known many of the most powerful men in this city since I was a kid. But shit, if you brought as much business to [this corporation] as I did, they'd have your name up in lights. I'm certain that the Senior VPs think it's all because of my dad."

The dilemma confronting all boss's sons is primarily an internal psychological struggle for appropriate recognition. They assume, quite correctly, that, coming from a background that purportedly provides them with a head start, they must be much more successful than others in order to derive comparable credit for their achievements.

Recall that success is defined in *relative* terms. A person is judged to be a success only if his achievements, regardless of their absolute quality, surpass the level of performance expected from his reference group. To be a success in America, one must *climb* from "rags to riches," or at least from the bottom rung of some ladder to the top. The individual who comes from a wealthy background must climb beyond his family's riches in order to get credit for what he has done. In essence, boss's sons must compensate for the "discounting" effects of "that which they have been given."

This "discounting effect" (or "discounting principle" as psychologists call it[5]) is the primary cause of the pain of the "Boss's Son Dilemma." It can be seen in a number of situations where there are very obvious explanations for desired outcomes apart from someone's personal or "inner" attributes such as personality or talent. For example, why was Judge Smith's son nominated for the vacant seat in Congress? Why did young, beautiful Barbara marry old millioniare Morton? The answers to these questions could very well be "merit" and "love," respectively, but observers would be more likely to assume that "influence" and "money" were the determining factors.

In essence, the crux of the dilemma is that with two plausible causes available to explain a particular outcome, the more salient of the two typically gets "credit." If your name is Kennedy or Getty, "who you are" is almost always much more salient that "what you did." Thus, your ability or efforts receive less credit for an outcome (nomination to a vacant Congressional seat) than would be the case if your name were Kagan or Green. A Kennedy who achieves an outcome identical to one achieved by a Kagan is also less likely to be judged a success.

## "IF YOU'RE SO SMART, HOW COME YOU'RE NOT RICH?"

We have seen that one of the more rewarding aspects of success is that it is a source of prestige, freedom, and power. Translated into operational terms, success would predictably result in a person's being judged more knowledgeable or informed than would otherwise be the case were it not for his success. A halo of wisdom radiates from those who have *earned* their way to the top. This is somewhat of a paradox to those who are *born* into successful families and are thus subjected to rigorous performance standards prior to being judged worthy or not. Yet those who have *achieved* success through an arduous climb to the top are presumed to be intelligent and, as a direct consequence, attain popularity, social prestige, and influence.

Prominent businesspeople are routinely subjected to this phenomenon when recruited to advise university presidents. Typically, the motivation behind asking these successful people to extend themselves beyond their principal area of expertise is not mercenary. Although it is undeniable that spaces on boards of directors are opened to businesspeople who will promise significant contributions to hospitals, colleges, and the like, organizations with no acute need for funds will, nevertheless, solicit the opinions of prominent executives.

We noted earlier that the "generalized respect" afforded those who are successful is, in large measure, a psychological artifact. Psychologists explain—by citing "implicit personality theories"—that when people judge each other on the basis of minimal data, they assume similar traits cluster together within an individual. Moreover, psychologists who have studied implicit personality theories find evidence among the lay public of the opinion that good attributes and bad attributes cluster independently in people.[6]

As we saw earlier, if you are successful in business it is *assumed* that you are generous and smart as well. If you are an investor who lost a family fortune through stock speculation, it would surprise no one if you were a slovenly bigot. Although we are all aware of countless exceptions to these "rules," one fundamental assumption remains operative despite contradictions: people who are successful (rich or powerful) are thought to possess a cornucopia of interrelated positive attributes. Because of this purely psychological perceptual bias, successful people make out like bandits!

Or do they? As we saw when examining the stress caused by success, people who are constantly forced to perform in accordance with increasing levels of aspiration (LOAs) frequently collapse under the strain of the performance requirements to which they must adhere. The upward spiral of expectations derived from continuous success creates performance demands that can cause stress responses identical to those that result from physical disasters.

The attribution of limitless abilities imposed upon successful people can also cause unremitting hassles. For Tevye, a poor, unknown, undervalued peasant, the prospects of being a rich man sought after for opinions and advice seemed like a dream too good to be true. For those who are already successful, the endless stream of sycophants they inevitably attract seems more like a disease than a dream. Even in situations where the suitors of a successful person are not servile, their assumptions of his wisdom, intelligence, and insight are typically burdensome and stressful.

Actress/journalist Candice Bergen is one successful woman who has had a lifelong battle against the expectations imposed upon her by being the daughter of a famous ventriloquist and, more significantly, strikingly beautiful. Like any form of natural ability or talent, beauty is a key to success and in many contexts (e.g., beauty contests) a criterion for success. In a manner identical to fame and money, beauty also imposes burdensome expectations upon those who possess it. As Candice Bergen observed:

> "People who don't have it think beauty is a blessing. Actually, it's a kind of sentence, a confinement. It sets you apart. People see you as an object, not as a person, *and they project a set of expectations into that object*" [emphasis added].[7]

In a variety of other contexts, not only the movies where "beautiful people" prevail, the burden of expectations can be seen inexorably to follow success. At all levels of athletic competition, the ones who finish second inevitably assert, "Wait until next year!," whereas champions are only looking forward to their vacation. Winners know that a "repeat performance" will be expected and that everyone in the league will be gunning for them. As current champions they are presumed to have a head start in next season's race—an unenviable position considering the fact that all entrants will be nipping at their heels. Moreover, all champions know that unless they retire —quit while they're ahead as the saying goes—anything less than back-to-back championships represents a subjective failure.

Politicians, traditionally immune to psychological pressures, balk at anything resembling "frontrunner," "leader," or "winner" status in election races until the final votes are cast. Avoidant behavior such as this is far more than good manners or superstitious behavior. Most politicians believe that acknowledging the lead in a political race is tantamount to committing political suicide. Why? Because frontrunners can be held up to higher standards than can others. They can be attacked for shortcomings identical to those inherent in various also-rans and be found culpable *because* they are likely victors. Democrats Kennedy and Carter proved this as they captured the presidency, firing pot shots at their incumbent Republican opponents with abandon throughout the electoral campaign. How soon they both learned, upon succeeding in their respective bids for the presidency, what different standards are set after a victory, and how what was proper for underdogs will not be tolerated in winners.

Businesses are particularly vulnerable to the differential set of expectations held up to leaders of industry as opposed to fledgling businessmen or upstart companies. Avis, exploiting Franklinesque downward self-promotion, gave Hertz hell by claiming that they were number 2 and trying harder. Implicit in the Avis ad campaign was the contention that number 1 Hertz was accountable to higher standards than number 2 Avis. Of course as number 2, Avis should be allowed minor flaws. Moreover, if Hertz was not performing much better than Avis, the only possible conclusion one could reach is that the "big guy" was really slipping. In a similar fashion, ever since advertising has come to accept personal attacks by one company against another, second-place colas have attacked the leader, Coke, while Burger King and Wendy's have attempted to burn McDonald's with their ads.

Thus, we see that those in first place or leadership positions, or holding star status, must exert a gargantuan effort simply to remain where they are, not to mention to make advances. Given the nature of their dilemma—being expected to outperform all others in the competition, and getting far less credit for their winning performances than would be the case if *they* were number two—one wonders why the allure of success is so appealing. It's as though being "second banana" is actually more comfortable. We can now understand that one of the features that makes being at the top so lonely is the absence of anyone to share the pressure of staying there. Many of those who have reached the top report that they miss something as fundamental as another human being who can praise them or comfort them *without* arousing suspicions.


## PROBLEMS RESULTING FROM PRAISE

In the Introduction, Moss Hart's and Tennessee Williams's reactions to success were contrasted so as to demonstrate the two-edged quality of this incredibly intense experience. Hart asserted that success made one feel more alive, while Williams maintained that success gave rise to "a kind of death." In particular, Williams claimed that as a result of the phenomenal success of *The Glass Menagerie*, his relationships with friends and other important people changed dramatically:

A well of cynicism rose in me. . . . Sincerity and kindliness seemed to have gone out of my friends' voices. I
suspected them of hypocrisy. . . . I was impatient of what
I took to be inane flattery.
    I got so sick of hearing people say, "I loved your play!"
that I could not say thank you any more. I no longer felt
any pride in the play itself but began to dislike it, probably
because I felt too lifeless ever to create another.[8]

Williams's reaction to his friends after the success of
*The Glass Menagerie*, while extreme in degree, was not extreme in terms of the kind of reactions known to follow
overwhelming success. The psychiatric community has long
been aware of the multitude of intense *negative* reactions
that follow success, and Williams's antisocial response pattern is one that is frequently observed. What is important
for the purposes of this discussion is to underscore the
fact that Williams's hostility had a particular target: his
friends' voices, their "inane flattery," the phrase "I loved
your play." In short, Williams had an extremely negative
reaction to the praise, or, more specifically, the positive
evaluative feedback he received once his play had become
successful and he was elevated to the status of "successful
playwright."
    The term "positive evaluative feedback" is used to
represent a broad class of reinforcements such as praise,
compliments, rewards, and awards.[9] Except in rare circumstances, the intention of positive evaluative feedback
is to inform an individual that he or she is in some way,
and for some reason, meritorious. Moreover, praise and
kudos are expected to elevate the mood of those who are
talented and fortunate enough to receive them. The problem, as we see from Williams's quote, is that despite its
intended effect, positive evaluative feedback can precipitate a host of unintended reactions in those to whom it is

directed. If we examine the nature of positive evaluative feedback and how it is conveyed from evaluators to those who are being evaluated ("target persons") we will be in a position to understand why reactions like those of Tennessee Williams occurred.

## CONFUSION AS TO THE MEANING AND INTENT OF FEEDBACK

There is no one form, style, or manner in which positive evaluative feedback is conveyed. Furthermore, positive evaluative feedback may result from any number of disparate events, even some that are beyond a target person's control, such as lineage. The only absolutely essential "defining feature" of positive evaluative feedback is that it provides two types of "messages" to target persons: information, and a message about control.[10]

The informational aspect of positive evaluative feedback is easy to understand. In the case of feedback derived from success, it typically indicates what was achieved, at what level(s) of competency, and, most important, by whom. "Congratulations, your November sales figure of $350,000 is the highest in our firm's history," is an example of the sort of unambiguous information that can be conveyed by positive evaluative feedback. This type of positive evaluative feedback provides a *"ranking,"* which is crucial for the experience of success.

The control aspect of positive evaluative feedback is more complex—and more problematic. This message reflects who has the power over the behavior in question—who, in essence, is responsible for a particular behavior's emergence. Feedback such as, "That brilliant proposal of yours really cinched the deal," both ranks a performance *and* indicates that the proposal writer gets most if not all of the credit for closing a particular contract. Similarly,

"The chocolate cake you've baked is so delicious, it ought to be illegal" tells the cook in question that the person feasting on cake is not an indiscriminate chocoholic. Instead, this person recognizes quality chocolate cakes and has singled out the baker's as being one of the best. More important, this particular instance of praise places unambiguous credit for the quality of the chocolate cake in the hands and mixing bowls of the target person.

There are essentially two ways in which positive evaluative feedback can cause pain and problems for successful people: (1) when the control component suggests that factors *external* to a target person's abilities or personal efforts may have accounted for success, and (2) when the informational component of the feedback fails to identify a target person's achievements. The disturbing result of both of these "problems" is that the successful target person is left questioning his "ownership" of success he thought was legitimately his own.

*How "Faulty" Praise Contributes to the "Boss's Son Dilemma:" Distortions in the Control Component of Positive Evaluative Feedback.* Not all positive evaluative feedback is presented in a manner that acknowledges the control of the person responsible for the performance being evaluated. Consider the following kudos: "Jerry, I told you you could close that deal. Congratulations! You've got the old 'Stevens charm' which has been with this company since your grandfather founded it over 35 years ago," or "Judy, you're the best female litigator in the firm. You've been incredibly effective in those sex discrimination cases we've been receiving." One of the clearest messages conveyed by both instances of positive evaluative feedback is the fact that forces *external* to the personal abilities or will-to-succeed of the target persons were responsible for the successful outcomes they achieved.

Succeeding because one is blessed with the "Stevens

charm," or because one is female and can handle "female" cases, places a huge asterisk or footnote on one's achievements. Both examples cited above serve notice to the target persons that attributes over which they had no control (a presumed genetic gift for social interaction or the correct gender) were at least partially responsible for their success.

Positive evaluative feedback that implies that factors such as one's heritage or sex contributed to the occurrence of a successful outcome is missing an important ingredient: what psychologists call "personalism."[11] Feedback that is not personalistic is perceived as being directed at an individual for reasons of his *ascribed status*—the social position someone occupies by reason of birthright. Positive evaluative feedback directed at one's *achieved status*—social ranking based on one's accomplishments—always has a more favorable impact.

Often, for high-status individuals, positive evaluative feedback appears to be *pro forma*. Stars who merely walk onto the stage of the *Tonight Show* receive applause; what did they do (that night) to deserve it? Keynote speakers will often receive more applause prior to their speech than following an authentic evaluation of their performance.

When a person succeeds owing to his "Stevens charm" or the fact that she is the best *female* litigator, the lack of personalism inherent in such feedback deprives the recipient from resting comfortably with the belief that he or she can reliably replicate successful performances under different circumstances. In addition, feedback lacking personalism is typically perceived as more transient than highly personalistic feedback. If you receive praise for who you are as opposed to what you do, you fear that on future occasions when audience attitudes may have changed slightly, your ability to succeed will have changed as well—for the worse.

Consider, for example, the "best female litigator" who wins case after case between 1980 and 1985. If the "female"

aspect of this positive evaluative feedback is as consequential as it sounds, this attorney will doubtless confront
the following insecurities when contemplating her future:
"Will I be as successful in 1990, when finding women attorneys in courtrooms is a common occurrence?" "Can I
be as successful with cases not involving sex discrimination, where a jury will not afford me sympathy for representing those of my gender who have been victimized?"
Similar doubt must plague the businessman with "charm"
inherited from his grandfather: "Maybe I couldn't make it
on the other coast where my family name is meaningless."
"Are they responding to the quality of my business
plan or the quality of the 50-year-old corporation that I
represent?"

The essence of the dilemma posed by positive evaluative feedback is that in order to feel secure in the belief
that the success is truly something that you "own" and
control, you must shed, disguise, or deny central aspects
of who you are if "who you are" can account for the feedback. In order for the businessman working in the family
business to know whether or not his business plans have
intrinsic worth, he might be forced to change the name
appearing on his proposals when they are submitted for
review. Similarly, if the prevailing bias favors female attorneys, the only way for a woman to get a totally unbiased
reading of her legal skills would be to disguise her sex or
have her petitions and briefs submitted by a male associate.

Returning to the example of the Kennedy children,
the two-edged quality of a successful heritage can be seen
with extreme clarity. These individuals are victimized by
overwhelming expectations imposed upon them as a consequence of being born into a family that has had more
than its fair share of extremely competent offspring. Thus,
while given many luxuries, they are expected to perform
in an exemplary fashion. Simultaneously, however, they

find it extremely difficult to derive full credit if and when they succeed. If a Kennedy child succeeds in gaining admission to Harvard, the prevailing "wisdom" would ascribe it to the family's ties to both the institution and its endowment. The same would hold true for a Kennedy who won elective office in Massachusetts: "He couldn't lose in this state with his name!"

When positive evaluative feedback makes it appear as though an individual's ascribed status accounted for a successful outcome, that person is functionally equivalent to a Kennedy being elected to Congress from Massachusetts. While he may have a strong desire to attribute his "win" to his own skills and tenacity, nagging doubts will inevitably persist. For praise, accolades, or kudos to have their intended impact, they must contain the message that success was solely a function of the performance under consideration, not the person's family name, gender, employer, or whatever. Occasionally, evaluations that fail to identify an individual's personal responsibility for a successful outcome may elicit pain rather than pleasure. Consider the following comments from Patti Davis—a woman who once aspired to be an actress, and happens to be Ronald Reagan's daughter:

> I would get a small part, just something to get experience . . . but the publicity would focus on me more than the star. Or I would get a call to read for a part, and then realize they just wanted to see what Reagan's daughter was like. It was humiliating.[12]

*"Are They Praising Me or My Play?" Distortions in the Informational Aspect of Positive Evaluative Feedback.* You will recall that Tennessee Williams, who called success a "kind of death," suspected his friends of hypocrisy and considered their praise of *The Glass Menagerie* to be "inane flattery." His aggravation and depression following the re-

lease of the play can now be understood as an extremely adverse reaction to positive evaluative feedback that did not convey the appropriate degree of personalism. Specifically, the praise expressed by Williams's friends failed to inform him that his play represented an achievement. This is not to say that Williams's friends *should* have behaved in a manner other than they did. On the contrary, their praise, as delivered, might have been appropriate. But something—what they said, how they said it, or why they said it—left the playwright bereft of positive feelings.

The human's need for positive evaluative feedback operates in a fashion that parallels our need for milk and sleep. From infancy to early childhood, we cannot get enough nurturance, milk, and sleep, and those in contact with children know to supply these necessities as often as possible. However, with appropriate maturation and growth, our needs become more differentiated. Proper development (both physical and psychological) depends upon limiting sleep and engaging in extended periods of exercise and education, which are essential to stimulating our bodies and minds. Similarly, our intake of milk must be limited and our diets must become diversified if we are to prosper physically and grow. Though we only initially require simple solid foods and milk for a healthy diet, later on our diets must become more complex. Not only do we require a wider range of nutrients, we also require a range of palate-pleasing tastes and types of meals to ensure that we eat in amounts necessary to maintain proper nutrition.

Our needs for different types and intensities of nurturance as well as positive evaluative feedback also change over time. It is safe to assume that younger children require massive amounts of unqualified approval from parents and relatives informing them that they are loved and deserve to be. However, as noted earlier, there comes a time when positive evaluative feedback must become highly qualified—or contingent on performance—for a child to develop a healthy sense of self-esteem. Parents must differentiate for their children when they have *performed* in an exemplary fashion as opposed to when they are loved for *being* who they are.

All of us have either experienced or observed the following scene: a teenager completes a recital (ball game, science fair) and is embraced by a parent who gushes, "Oh Jake, you are so wonderful." The clearly uncomfortable child is next overheard remarking, "Oh big deal [Mom, Dad]. Of course your gonna say that; you're my [Mom, Dad]." Although scenes with an entirely opposite conclusion are also common—children bursting with pride because they have pleased their parents—it is strange that the initial scene depicting the uncomfortable recipient of parental praise is so familiar to us all. Who better to receive accolades from than someone whose love is unfailing? For many, the answer to this question is "almost anyone!"

Parents, like some employers or supervisors, are frequently judged to be extremely poor sources of positive evaluative feedback, particularly when they are perceived as being "interdependent others."[13] Occupying the status of "interdependent other" vis-à-vis a target person means simply that the "other's" welfare, quality of life, or outcome satisfaction is inextricably linked to the outcomes of a target person. The most obvious example of this relationship exists between a "stage mother" and her child. Leaving aside the question of whether or not the child is pushed to perform, one fact is undeniable: the actual fortunes of the mother-and-child "team" are ultimately a function of the child's ability to perform. If the child does well and receives lucrative bookings, both mother and child prosper; if the child's performances are failures, both suffer.

The question facing us is how praise from a stage

mother (an interdependent other) affects her child. Regardless of the love that exists between the child and his mother, the financial aspect will always affect their relationship. Given the fact that the child's successes serve to enhance the quality of both their lives, "Son, you did great!" has a different meaning than would be the case if it was said by a priest to one of his Sunday school students. From stage mother to son, "great," "nice job," or "fine piece of work," can be construed as being an exhortation to be productive so that both parties will live comfortably.

In those circumstances where interdependency is high, the objectivity of the dependent party vanishes. His perspective and objectivity would be severely compromised by his personal investment in having the performance turn out to be a success.

The justifiable assumption that stage mothers (and fathers) would be biased in favor of judging their child's performances to be successful presumes no malice or conscious distortion on their part. The same sort of bias manifests itself in hometown crowds at athletic events. In fact, sports teams thrive on biases of this sort, and often depend on the blind passion of fans for morale boosts during trying times.

The difference between sports fans and stage mothers, and why one bias is helpful and the other a hindrance, lies in each one's respective share of outcomes. Even if we acknowledge that fans bet on sporting events, it is clearly the case that the primary benefit they derive from their team's victory is intrinsic satisfaction. Through an identification with "the hometown boys," they *feel* good when their team is triumphant; their payoff is primarily psychological. Not so for stage mothers. In many instances, their standard of living is yoked to the quality of their child's performances. This is not to say that pride in their child or vicarious fulfillment are not contributing factors in a stage mother's motivation; they often are. But the fact that material well-being is frequently a large part of the relationship between stage mother and child has an immutable influence upon how expressions of positive evaluative feedback are perceived.

The target person receiving praise from an interdependent other experiences a dilemma. The words *sound* right but the message *feels* inauthentic. In its most extreme form, the situation of the target person is comparable to the john who is called "darling" or "dear" by the prostitute. The fact that financial interdependence is the tie that binds the two in a relationship permanently distorts the information that might otherwise be construed as positive evaluative feedback.

## ALONE AT "THE TOP," SURROUNDED BY SUSPICIONS

Relationships are rarely as well-defined as those existing between stage mothers and their offspring or prostitutes and their johns. This makes the dilemmas encountered by successful people all the more pronounced. On the one hand, once you become successful *everyone* close to you assumes some attributes of an interdependent other since your success can surely benefit them. If a politician gets elected to office, he can assist virtually all of his cronies in some fashion. Likewise for the successful artist. Once you become the "darling" of the media, invitations to all the "right" events start pouring in, benefiting both the artist and his entourage.

I believe that Tennessee Williams suffered from this dilemma. Once *The Glass Menagerie* became a success, he was catapulted into a position of extreme power, which rendered virtually all of his friends "one down" in terms of prominence and influence. Furthermore, his inner circle would all benefit from his power if he chose to exercise it.

The fact that he became empowered to affect the quality of his friends' lives cost him the sense of satisfaction he might otherwise have derived from their praise. As he said, "Sincerity and kindliness seemed to have gone out of my friends' voices [following the success of my play]." If there is a sense that kudos are merely a form of "kissing up" to someone who can benefit you, they leave the target person as empty as a john looking for affection from a prostitute.

Executives are frequently the victims of interdependent others, particularly when they hold the positions of president and CEO. Corporate protocol suggests deference to executive officers by those beneath them in the organizational hierarchy, and common sense demands it. If this principle is operative and you happen to be atop the pyramid, whom do you turn to for honest feedback? Where can you turn for evaluations of your work or business plans and feel confident that you will receive unbiased judgments? Certainly not to those who serve in the organization, which in certain corporations means virtually everyone save the board or, in the case of corporate presidents, the CEO.

Executives and award-winning artists are both deprived the satisfactions of those close to them because they are aware of the manner in which interdependency influences judgments of competence and quality. Even if we assume that a subordinate wants to provide a corporate CEO with honest, unbiased judgments, can the executive believe the praise of someone who *needs* his good will?

Probably not, which is why many successful people suffer as Tennessee Williams did. They find that their success has placed them in a position where they can't depend upon valued people for accurate readings of "the lay of the land." Paradoxically, many executives who control the workings of huge corporations lose control over an incredibly important aspect of their lives: the validity of the feedback they receive. The distress caused by this paradoxical state of affairs can only be eliminated if the executive either disguises the origins of his work or seeks counsel outside of his corporation. Considering the fact that much of what an executive would need feedback on constitutes privileged information, there are a limited number of external sources to whom this beleaguered individual can turn.

At a minimum, we now see that positive evaluative feedback from an interdependent other creates two precursors to psychological stress. On the one hand, the target person interprets it as a demand for high-level performance rather than a ranking along an evaluative continuum. (From our definition of stress, we know that stress derives from excessive performance demands.) In addition, we see that the questionable positive evaluative feedback he receives from interdependent others deprives him of any control over the information he receives. Again, according to the definition of stress, lacking control over aspects of your life is a major precursor to stress.

It is obvious that most successful people do not react as strongly to the stress created by "suspect" positive evaluative feedback as Tennessee Williams did. Most find among their associates "confidants" whom they can trust for veridical feedback. Nevertheless, the "stress of success" conveyed by expectations and praise can be quite severe. The next chapter will describe the most widely recognized psychiatric disorders resulting from success.

Successful people can become victims of success for a variety of reasons. Central among these is the fact that expectations and praise are often showered on them or their children independent of their actual performances. When an individual's ascribed status—the role he occupies because of who he is as opposed to what he does—determines performance demands and praise, the burden of expectations can create stress responses identical to those deriving from physical disasters or disease. Pressures from success can lead to drug abuse and suicide, as we have noted in children from successful families. And many successful individuals report dissatisfactions resulting from the difficulty they have in trusting the opinions of others *after* they have become important or powerful.

The successful person's problems are made worse by the fact that the most direct means of shedding inappropriate expectations and obtaining positive evaluative feedback for his performances is to deny or disguise who he is. Like the "poor little rich girl" who must hide her family name if she is to be certain that suitors are not gold diggers, the successful person is destined to encounter excessive pressure and insincerity in others unless or until he can function incognito. When successful people cannot extricate themselves from their lineage, rank, or history of success, more extreme forms of "escape" such as withdrawal through alcohol abuse or depression are common. The upcoming chapters will explore the specific psychiatric disorders resulting from the stresses inherent in The Success Syndrome.

Part Three

# THOSE WRECKED BY SUCCESS

## Chapter Seven

# "SOCIAL" DISORDERS CAUSED BY SUCCESS

*Envy is a pain of mind that successful men cause their neighbors.*

Onasander

One defining feature of success noted throughout this book is that judging someone to be a "success" must involve some form of comparison with his peers. Being successful does not necessarily involve being the "best," "biggest," or "most" something on the face of the earth; one must merely excel along an evaluative continuum that includes comparable individuals whose performances can serve as points of comparison. One can be considered successful if he is the best student in his grade, in his school, in his state, or in his field, be it medicine or medieval history. The ranking that leads to the experience of success means simply that he has outperformed or ranked higher in measurable terms than anyone in relevant comparison groups.

Earlier discussions of what consequences await those who have "made it to the top" focused primarily on the fact that, generally speaking, one is rewarded for excelling relative to one's peers. If we examine the consequences that are likely to befall "the best student" as his career proceeds from grade school to the professional world, it is safe to assume that he will be singled out for a variety of academic awards, scholarships, cash prizes, and, eventually, appointments on prestigious boards and councils. Those who excel at their "trade" can expect to receive a

great many tangible indicators of being ahead of the pack
or, as Merrill Lynch would say, "A Breed Apart." Occasionally, however, those who are successful note that being
*set apart* is the most noticeable consequence of their
achievements. Frequently, it is one that they would rather
do without.

Earlier I introduced the concept of the "evil eye" as
one of the detrimental consequences of becoming successful. To all, including the most casual observer, it is
apparent that jealousy, resentment, and even physical acts
of aggression are an almost inevitable "cost" of succeeding.
Joseph with his coat of many colors and the murderer Cain
are biblical figures who provide unambiguous examples
of the extremes to which others—even family members—
will go to vent their ill will toward those who have been
successful. Whether we assume that the achievements of
successful people serve as irritants to the "average"—re-
minding them of their limitations—or assume that jealous
people lacking the rewards of success merely want them
denied to all, the fact remains that the successful individual
has a real problem to cope with when confronting evil
eyes, or the malevolence behind dirty looks.

The successful who can persuade themselves to believe the childhood refrain, "sticks and stones will break
my bones but words will never hurt me," are fortunate
since they will retain their psychological health. Yet many
successful people—the more seasoned ones—refuse to believe that words cannot hurt them, having witnessed the
devastation that can be caused by gossip, lies, rumors, and
innuendos.

Even on those occasions when the jealousy engen-
dered by one's becoming "a breed apart" brings nothing
more than passive rejection, the cost to the successful person can be devastating. There is no need to embellish on

the pain of loneliness; one health statistic will suffice: un-married men are reported to have a life expectancy that is 10 years *less* than that of their married counterparts. Leav-ing aside the question of whether it is or is not life-short-ening, social isolation is, with rare exception, always ex-traordinarily painful.

Despite the burgeoning phenomenon of gourmet din-ners-for-one packaged for yuppies, we are a couple- or group-oriented society. Man is a social animal who needs others to help define reality, validate feelings, and provide psychological security against a world fraught with capri-cious and uncontrollable events. Those who go it alone typically suffer and fail.

Take the bizarre story of Howard Hughes as an ex-ample. This man, who earned millions, died a crazed re-cluse. Despite his gargantuan efforts to use his money as a means of insulating himself from the stress and hassles of normal life, it is apparent, from all reports, that "life" got to him anyway. While no one can say, for certain, what Hughes's life was like once he began his isolation, we can presume that it was not gratifying. He showed himself to be a prime example of the fact that if success means losing contact with others and being alone, success must be "no damn good at all." If we examine the success-sabotaging behavior of many *potentially* successful people, we can see that many young people are aware of the pain inherent in social isolation born of success—a fact appar-ently lost on the late Mr. Hughes.


## ACADEMIC UNDERACHIEVEMENT

To a child between the ages of 6 and 16, "teacher's pet" or "bookworm" are among the worst things that one can be called. In some school settings, these slurs have an effect equivalent to that of contracting leprosy: the "contaminated" individual is ostracized. To combat these slurs and to avoid social isolation, many brilliant children will fail to perform at a level teachers and test scores would predict of them. These underachievers are the youngest population known to suffer the effects of The Success Syndrome.

Several scientists who have studied academic underachievers are unequivocal in their conclusion that this mode of juvenile self-sabotage is an attempt to avoid slapping one's peers in the face and suffering social isolation.[1] Research on this type of behavior documents that underachievers will not only actively distort test performances so as to score lower than they know they can, but will also behave in a socially self-sabotaging manner when in the company of adults.

In an effort to be "one of the gang," academic underachievers are known to actively reject the favorable attention of teachers by advocating attitudes that are contrary to those that might elicit a "teacher's pet" status. Underachievers fear that were they to receive positive recognition from authority figures, the value of their "stock" in their peer group would drop precipitously. Instead, they create behavioral problems requiring negative attention from the school guidance department. Chronic truancy is another common symptom of academic underachievement. What is harder to document—but far more consequential— is the psychological suffering caused by the conflict generated by the opposing influences of peers advocating conformity and adults advocating success and maximum achievement.

Several brilliant young underachievers were referred to me for "executive stress" therapy by psychotherapists who recognized that the emotional problems of these adolescents were virtually identical to those of stressed corporate CEOs. They understood that both groups suffer the aversive consequences of social isolation. Academic underachievers (like CEOs alone at the top) are stressed in the classical sense of the word, since they must confront performance expectations that they cannot possibly meet. To behave in a fashion that would ensure the approval of those their own age means to fail themselves and defy the expectations conveyed by society; to succeed means to endure some degree of social isolation. Their plight may be characterized as akin to being between a rock and a hard place; they are damned if they do achieve and damned if they don't.

*"I Told You So!"* The final irony of the underachiever's plight is experienced when and if he attempts to live up to his potential. In one systematic study of underachieving boys, respondents noted that an acknowledgment of their abilities, and performances in line with their capabilities, would "portend longer and more difficult assignments from teachers, and greater dissatisfactions in parents with a boy's current achievement status."[2] Stated another way, were an underachiever ever to decide to perform as expected, he would encounter the dubious reward of higher and more burdensome performance expectations and parents who, when presented with "potential-consistent" academic performances, would self-righteously proclaim, "I told you so; we knew you could do it all along."

In this circumstance, improved performance is actually a type of punishment. Instead of receiving credit for turning a losing performance record around, the now-successful child has a new problem to contend with. In a manner of speaking, becoming successful is a tacit admission of not having tried or of intentionally failing in the past.[3] An admission of laziness or sabotage might warrant actual chastisement. The net result of this dilemma for the underachieving child is a lifetime of substandard performance unless the prevailing climate of parental opinion shifts to welcome rather than punish performances that confirm their child's innate abilities.

In our previous discussion of the way in which "head starts" in life can deprive an individual of the credit he *could* receive for successful performances, we considered the protagonist from the movie *Five Easy Pieces*. Jack Nicholson's portrayal of this tortured soul also served to illustrate the manner in which a family member's "I told you so!" serves to destroy the motivation of an individual tentatively attempting to live up to his potential. In the case of the Nicholson character, each time he played the piano in earnest, the person he played for expressed a double-edged compliment, something to the effect of either: "That was great; why haven't you been playing all along?" or "It's a pity you've been wasting such great talents." The thinly veiled criticism inherent in compliments like these is what deters many talented individuals from pursuing success in a career already occupied by an opinionated family member.

## STATUS INCONSISTENCY: "DO I BELONG DOWN ON THE FARM OR IN PAREE?"

It is often the case that a person can "run with the pack" during his formative years, and only later in life achieve successes that differentiate him from the crowd. When success in adulthood forces a person to physically and psychologically abandon his "roots"—ties with his friends, activities, styles of behaving, and neighborhood—the negative psychological and physical effects of this change can range from alcoholism and schizophrenia to coronary heart disease.[4] The technical name for this situation is "status inconsistency." This condition frequently imposes costs severe enough to force a high-powered achiever to choose between his health or his career.

Status inconsistency refers to situations wherein a person's position or standing in a variety of sociocultural groupings deviates greatly. An example of someone who is "status inconsistent" would be a physician who was raised, and treats only Medicare patients, in the Louisiana bayou. This individual is thought to have a low socioeconomic status and a high occupational status. The specific type of status inconsistency that concerns us, "achievement inconsistency," occurs whenever an individual's accomplishments place him in the "fast lane" despite the fact that he grew up, and is both attitudinally and psychologically rooted, on dirt roads.

One of the most stressful aspects of achievement inconsistency is that "back home" and "the fast lane" both provide their own unique rewards while requiring sets of mutually exclusive behaviors. The clothes, manner, and even language required of the urban sophisticate are guaranteed to put off the "hometown boys." Similarly, the demeanor accepted by the working class would never be tolerated in the boardroom of a Fortune 500 corporation.

One of the more well-publicized episodes of achievement inconsistency was that of James Earl Carter's presidency. Throughout his often ill-fated administration, this superachieving man from the tiny town of Plains, Georgia, was forced to balance the conflicting demands of his rural background and the status he acquired in the most powerful and prestigious elective office in the world.

Carter, who referred to himself as "Jimmy" (not the formal-sounding James), was accused of failing to effect public policy because he never learned how to deal with Congress—a fact attributed to his inability or unwillingness to conform to the social mores of Washington, D.C. A clear and sadly comic example of Carter's conflicts was embodied in "brother Billy," whose beer guzzling and public rowdiness cost his brother public relations points as well as extensive psychological distress.

At this point in time, it is probably not possible to document the actual toll taken on Carter by his efforts to cope with his achievement inconsistency. Nevertheless, most competent political observers would consider it undeniable that this brilliant politician failed some of the more crucial tests of his presidency because he refused, or was unable, to accommodate to the style of "Washington insiders."

Status inconsistents are found in every walk of life. From the small-town sports hero who is both shocked and scared by the fast pace of the "big leagues," to the shy science whiz whose genius catapults him into a corporate presidency, success often precipitates psychological conflicts that pit an individual's former demeanor against his current style. Individuals who suffer from status inconsistency are by no means fakes or flashes in the pan. Rather, they are truly talented individuals torn between conflicting life-styles. Desirous of accommodating two different "worlds," they suffer the stress of attempting an almost impossible juggling act.

The positive aspects of the two incompatible statuses that give rise to achievement inconsistency can create what psychologists call "approach–approach" conflicts. When an individual is confronted with two attractive but conflicting alternatives (e.g., family versus career), choosing one "approach" almost always means foregoing the other.

People typically force themselves to choose one of the two alternatives and go on with their productive lives. However, as noted earlier, when both of the pulls are strong and both resist abandonment—say, for example, a career change that promises a six-figure income versus a nurturant hometown environment that has been yours for 35 years—the conflicts that ensue have been known to cause severe psychological distress or what is commonly referred to as a "nervous breakdown." On the brink of these "breakdowns" (more typically bouts of alcoholism, severe depression, anxiety disorders, or even coronary heart disease), people often reject the conflict-inducing successes they thought would bring them only happiness and joy.

The most poignant example of this dilemma is seen in many successful women between the ages of roughly 30 and 36. These women often confront an "approach–approach" conflict born of a type of status inconsistency that can truly create an irresolvable problem. I am referring to the inconsistency born of corporate goals that often eschew motherhood in the upper-executive ranks, and a woman's desire to bear children. The desire to enjoy the status of both worlds must frequently be abandoned in the face of what psychologists euphemistically call "reality concerns."

The reality for many women is that they are thwarted from achieving success in both realms because of the costs involved in attempting to walk a fine line between the two. The variations on this theme are limitless, but the outcome is often the same: the expectations and obligations derived from success in the corporate world are often incompatible with the necessities inherent in bearing a child.

Enlightened social and corporate policies are having a favorable impact on this situation, and women are finding it easier to fulfill simultaneously family and career aspirations. But a number of women still find that to make it in one world, they must abandon the other. This goes for marriage and a career as well as motherhood. Unfortunately, when neither a woman's external reality (job) nor internal motivation (biological clock) can be altered, the solution to her dilemma involves the painful necessity of dropping one aspiration or the other.

In most instances when an individual is forced to make this sort of choice as a result of harboring incompatible goals, a major depression will follow. In the next chapter we will explore another example of the way in which success can be instrumental in precipitating a psychological depression.

## Chapter Eight

# "WHERE DO I GO FROM HERE?"

## Depressions following Success

*In this world there are only two tragedies. One is not getting what one wants and the other is getting it.*
Oscar Wilde

Climbing the ladder of success to reach the top rung is the most commonly used metaphor for pursuing a career goal. From it we derive the colloquial expressions that refer to "success," including "reaching the top," "the top," or "arriving." Rarely do we find people who consider the initial stages of the process leading to success—"climbing"—as having the same value or potential for reward as attaining the goal. Why should they? To achieve a truly valuable goal, one must climb a ladder splintered with severe trials and tribulations. (Recall Spinoza's thought: "All excellent things are as difficult as they are rare.") Who wants to dwell upon hardships once your rewards are in hand?

The number of successful people who do wax nostalgic about the hard times they had would surprise those readers who have not experienced The Success Sydrome. In my clinical practice, I have found that many successful individuals, most notably entrepreneurs and athletes, talk fondly about their climb to the top and the difficulties they encountered along the way. Their stories go well beyond the travel advertisement that "getting there is half the fun." For a significant number of individuals wrecked by success, the road to their dream was a joyous struggle capped by an anxiety-ridden letdown once they arrived.

During the initial phases of psychotherapy with these successful people, it is quickly discovered that this sense of disappointment derives from the absence of goals. These people enter psychotherapy plagued by a variety of self-doubts and questions that can be categorized into two closely related groupings: "Where do I go from here?" or "What do I do for an encore?" In addition, and most significant, the fact that these successful people cannot find appropriate answers to these questions has resulted in their becoming clinically depressed. Their symptoms are identical to those commonly observed in the "classic" depressions precipitated by aversive events such as a major loss—death of a loved one and breakup of a marriage—or failure. They suffer from chronic lethargy, disrupted sleep patterns, and loss of appetite, self-esteem, and sex drive. The unique attribute of my patients, however, is that their symptoms of depression occur as a consequence of attaining success.

## LOSSES CONTAINED WITHIN SUCCESS

Many people who suffer "success depression," as the disorder has come to be called, sit atop the ladder of success looking around for a direction to their life. They are experiencing the sad realization that by achieving their goals, many aspects of their daily patterns of living will be ended or changed forever. In an extremely important way, individuals who suffer "success depression" are identical to those suffering from "classic" depression in that both experience a type of loss. For the "success depressive," it is almost always the case that success is like a game of gin rummy: to get something valuable for your "game plan" (an achievement or a particular card), something must be given up or discarded. Often that "something" was once valuable to the person discarding it, and typically is still valuable to others playing different "hands."

Examples of this "discard when you get" dilemma are all around us in varying degrees. The most common example occurs when a person finds a mate after years of dating. Few anticipate the losses that occur once this longed-for goal has been realized.

When an individual becomes half of a "couple," a number of freedoms are typically forfeited. Access to activities with "the boys" or "the girls" along with hobbies and other solitary pursuits must typically be subordinated to the needs of one's mate. Gone too is the freedom to act in the immature or irresponsible manner of being "footloose and fancy free." Spending—on clothing, spectator sports, fancy cars—is easier when *not* planning for a future. So too are vocational demands. Being undereducated or underemployed is acceptable for "kids" not yet leading adult lives.

When one finds a mate, a very significant aspect of the life one led in pursuit of that goal ends: dating. The implications of this are many. At a minimum, finding a mate means a reduction in the number of *novel* experiences (good or bad) one is exposed to. More significant, dating is an incredibly complex pattern of social interaction capable of providing single people with confirmation of their intelligence, wit, beauty, sex appeal, and desirability from multiple sources on an ongoing basis. It is not unreasonable to assume that attractive singles can be reinforced by a different person each time they attend a social gathering. While searching for "Mr. Right," a talented and beautiful single woman can hear that she is "Ms. Right" from countless men who are close to but "not quite" her ideal. Contrast this with the circumstances of a married woman, who would be looked upon disapprovingly for constantly evoking such praise.

Women who have devoted themselves to assuming the primary responsibility for raising a family often feel quite severely the pain of simultaneous achievement and loss. Should they succeed in raising healthy children able to leave home for college, careers, or to start their own families, the homemaker's sense of arriving atop some ladder of success is nothing if not bittersweet. Where can she go to apply her unique nurturing, instructional, and managerial skills? A mother's work product is delivered with love and cannot be easily transferred to another "project," if at all.

Psychotherapists share a similar dilemma. After working through extremely difficult and often painful times with an individual whom they have grown to care for quite intensely, they must say good-bye when that person is at his or her "best." Despite the fact that the expressed goal of a therapeutic relationship is to bid the patient farewell once he or she is no longer encumbered by psychological difficulties or distress, there is pain and ambivalence in these separations. The bittersweet aspect of each psychotherapeutic success is that the therapist must let go of the patient to make the success complete. In so doing, the therapist is deprived of sharing in the patient's gains and growth, to which he contributed so very much during the therapeutic relationship.

Athletes and entrepreneurs are the other professionals who, by virtue of the way in which they succeed, usually suffer a loss upon reaching a goal. Prior to reaching their goals, they are exposed to numerous ongoing opportunities for rewards. Every game can engage an athlete in a series of struggles enabling him to derive proof of his prowess. Every at bat or every shot at the basket can provide reinforcement for those with the skills to get a hit or sink the ball. Yet the sad irony of the athlete's world is that should he and/or his team be successful, a championship season ends immediately after the ultimate victory has been realized. What do these competitors look forward to during the "off-season" that can rival the camaraderie, daily reinforcements, fame, and positive anticipation of victory that were so stimulating during their pursuit of the championship ring, flag, or cup?

Similarly, the entrepreneur who, by definition, undertakes to *start* or *develop* a business enterprise, must view his project's success as a form of completion or ending. While in the process of developing an enterprise, the entrepreneur is always keeping a number of balls in the air. Negotiations with financiers, marketing representatives, research and development experts, and lawyers are all part of initiating business ventures that provide opportunities for the entrepreneur to demonstrate—and be rewarded for—a myriad of abilities. However, should he prove to be successful in shepherding an infant or invalid enterprise to the point it becomes profit-making, his entrepreneurial skills are no longer needed. Often a management team will be moved in to *sustain* what the entrepreneur has built, while he, if fortunate, moves on to another challenging project. Without the proper attitudes about his work and himself, many a successful entrepreneur moves on to psychotherapy.

The preceding illustrations describing how successful careers can subject a person to losses exemplify patients I have actually treated for success depression. Each of these success depressives, like many I am treating today, spent countless months or years searching for a way to find the kinds of reinforcers or rewards they had been experiencing up until achieving their success. The reinforcers or rewards ranged from many simple hugs, compliments, or thank-yous, to significant accolades and financial remuneration; yet the problem was still the same. The attractive "singles," homemakers, psychotherapists, athletes, and entrepreneurs, who had successfully achieved their personal or career goals, suffered from the fear they had lost sources of gratification that could never be replaced. Their "where do I go from here?" question was posed in an attempt to *actually* locate relationships or settings where they might possibly reestablish reinforcing relationships comparable to those that had existed during the hard times of struggling toward their goal.

Another group that traditionally experiences losses in conjunction with success are people facing retirement. For people who have been successful at their vocations, the final accomplishment of their career—reaching a time when they can reflect upon the consistency and quality of their work—is frequently a time when depression sets in. Many executives who had rarely been sick throughout their careers "suddenly" suffer chronic disorders in anticipation of retirement. Others simply refuse to retire, knowing that they cannot enjoy the riches they earned and *thought* they would have enjoyed when they had first been employed.

Outsiders who see these men and women working well past the point of financial security often characterize them as greedy or money hungry. They are dead wrong. What few outsiders recognize is that most successful older executives are working to fend off the depression and feelings of worthlessness that dominate their thoughts once they cease to prove on an ongoing basis that they are competent and effective.

The sense of power and control lost when an executive with extensive administrative responsibilities retires can be devastating. Having a staff report to you, control over the fate of your workers, and a sense of mastery over the fate of your life, provide, as discussed in an earlier chapter, one of the most positive feelings that derive from success. This feeling of mastery—which begins in early childhood and can extend indefinitely—is at the heart of the sense of self-satisfaction that people typically feel following success. If you can imagine the happiness that would result from having this feeling for a long time, you can begin to understand the devastation that occurs when it is taken away against your will. The resulting feeling is so painful that several of the patients I treated swore that to have avoided retirement—and the concomitant loss of mastery which followed—they would have gladly worked without a salary had they been able to retain their positions of power.

Many executives who are forced to retire, and so have power wrested from their grasp, cope with this loss through adaptive responses such as participation in programs like SCORE (Service Corps of Retired Executives) or other volunteer agencies that channel their skills for useful projects. Those who are not able to find appropriate forums in which to manifest their competencies experience a sense of *powerlessness* or *loss of control* over important aspects of their world. The consequences of these feelings are inevitably the same. Psychologists and psychiatrists have proven that the most common cause of depressions that are not the result of biochemical imbalances is the experience of hopelessness or the belief that one is helpless to control important outcomes.[1]

It is almost impossible to overstate the benefits that feeling "in control" can provide to one's life, or the devastation that can be wrought by feeling "out of control." Countless scientific studies have linked the experience of feeling out of control to the incidence of stress and depression. Researchers studying both disorders have documented that people are *less* affected by *what* happens to them than by *how* it occurred.[2] If an individual expects difficult working conditions, natural disasters, interpersonal difficulties, or other negative outcomes and is prepared for them psychologically, their impact on his health and well-being will be minimized. On the other hand, when events—either bad *or* good—occur without a person's being able to regulate their occurrence or prepare for their impact, the effect is negative and greater than would have been the case had the individual experienced some sense of control.

As reflected in the preceding discussion, success can often be the cause of losing control over positive outcomes. When this occurs, the result is no different from that which would be expected if the loss were from a disaster: depression ensues.

Many individuals who were formerly successful suffer similar depressions. They too experience a loss of control, but in their case it is over positive outcomes they would *like to earn*. Often, former successes can't control the flow of rewards they receive from past achievements; many receive more than they feel they deserve. The cruel paradox of this unique "loss of control" is that the consequence can be identical to a depression caused by ongoing success.

## "WASN'T HE GREAT!?!": THE PAIN OF REWARDS INDEPENDENT OF INSTRUMENTAL BEHAVIOR

In certain circumstances, the careers of businesspeople and professional athletes being prime examples, a successful person will receive a variety of reinforcers independent of his present level of functioning. Joe DiMaggio is still asked for autographs from fans—a manifestation of respect and caring that is highly reinforcing—

despite the fact that he retired from baseball about 30 years ago. In addition, he still receives financial remuneration because of baseball skills that ranked him as one of the greatest professional athletes of modern times. I am not referring here to deferred salary from the New York Yankees, but to the income garnered from his Mr. Coffee promotions. Cases such as his demonstrate that although success may occasionally involve the loss of certain reinforcers, on numerous other occasions it sets up conditions wherein rewards will be accrued well past the point that their being "earned" is completely comprehensible to the successful person.

DiMaggio and the rest of the nation probably realize there is no shortage of announcers who could read Mr. Coffee ad copy with greater clarity, gusto, and salesmanship than he. Equally apparent is the fact that there are few living heroes in America given as much reverence as is DiMaggio. Since advertising strives to achieve a positive "product identification" by pairing merchandise with desired images (heroes, beautiful scenes or people), DiMaggio's status as a former star athlete with high ethical standards, who also happened to marry one of the sexiest movie stars of all time, is a Madison Avenue dream.

Yet leaving aside the desires of Madison Avenue for a moment, we should note that surviving on the basis of past glories is not a uniformly rewarding experience for ex-stars. Being a former star and hearing "wasn't he great" sends a mixed message that can be quite painful. The paradox and double-edged quality inherent in "wasn't he great" is that it also states, quite clearly, "he's not great now."

To fully understand why messages of "wasn't he great" can "cut both ways," it is important to recognize the psychological distinction between *instrumental* and *consumptive* behaviors. *Instrumental behaviors* are goal-directed, intentional acts by which an individual purposefully moves to-

ward acquiring a desired outcome or goal. Climbing a tree
to pick an apple or driving one's car to the store for the
morning paper are examples of simple instrumental acts.
Careers are more complex patterns of instrumental behaviors that lead to multiple outcomes: money, prestige, power,
freeedom from boredom, and a sense of satisfaction. This
last outcome—personal satisfaction, also called self-efficacy[3]—is the most important derivative of instrumental
behavior. It is the one that informs you of your power to
control aspects of the world and the things within it that
ensure your safety, comfort, and happiness. To some degree, it is a by-product of all effective instrumental behaviors. Yet significant feelings of self-efficacy are derived only
from the kinds of actions that require such skill and ability
that they lead to noteworthy successes.

Consumptive behaviors, on the other hand, consist of
using the rewards derived from attaining one's goals. Eating the apple you picked or reading the morning paper
are examples of simple consumptive behaviors. Spending
one's salary, royalties, or pension are examples of consumptive behaviors that are guaranteed to be more involved than apple-eating or paper-reading since the range
of outcomes affected by one's salary or the like—mortgage
payments, utility bills, food—is more diversified.

The psychological distinction between instrumental
versus consumptive behaviors is captured with exquisite
insight by the Oriental proverb cited earlier: "If you *give*
a hungry man a fish, you can keep him alive. If you *teach*
a hungry man to fish, you give him a livelihood." In the
former case, the one typifying consumptive behavior, the
goal—to prevent starvation—is achieved, but without last-
ing effects. The hungry man will soon be hungry again,
with no greater likelihood of satisfying his hunger than
prior to receiving the gift of fish. Moreover, we can assume
that he would soon desire another fish from his one-time
benefactor, thereby making him dependent.

Teaching a man *to fish*, on the other hand, represents the instrumental orientation. Instead of creating a dependency, you provide the hungry man with a skill enabling him to assume the role of provider for himself as well as others. But most important, by teaching a man to fish you give him two good feelings: one derived from the means he can acquire for himself, and one from the confidence he acquires vis-à-vis the world. A man with instrumental skills feels that he can control parts of the world and, in a meaningful way, determine his fate. He also feels competent each and every time he executes an instrumental behavior and achieves a goal. As you will recall from our discussion of the psychological precursors to feeling successful, a sense of positive self-esteem—the feeling that one is competent to bring about a desired outcome—is the feeling inherent in those who enjoy pleasure and happiness from success.

Returning to the circumstances of former stars who receive "wasn't he great" feedback and rewards for what they once were, we can now see clearly that they are being *given* fish, not being taught, or asked, to fish. They are getting the rewards appropriate to those who are successful at *executing* instrumental behaviors, while they themselves are not doing what others without star status must do in order to receive comparable reinforcement. In effect, the reinforcements that follow "wasn't he great" accolades are not under the control of formerly successful people, and consequently often lead to depression.

## NONCONTINGENT SUCCESS

The type of success experienced by individuals rewarded for prior achievements is one instance of what psychologists call "noncontingent success" experiences. Noncontingent success refers to a range of positive outcomes that are not subject to personal control. In essence, the outcomes occur independent of an individual's instrumental behaviors. Instead of *achieving* noncontingent success, people find they are *receiving* it for attributes such as personal beauty, family ties, or status derived from past successes.[4]

From the perspective of the former great receiving noncontingent success, the most debilitating aspect of the experience comes from one's *interpretation* of the rewards or praise received. My clinical experience with victims of noncontingent success revealed that the thoughts accompanying receipt of noncontingent success are often on the order of, "They like [my family; my looks; the way I played ball], and are giving me these kudos [rewards] because of that—not for what I have done to earn kudos [rewards]." When this occurs, the individual receiving noncontingent success—like the starving man given a fish—is a consumer, failing to control or master his world through instrumental behavior, indebted to those who have given him things, and in all likelihood, depressed.

In the Introduction, I noted that former astronaut Buzz Aldrin was a classic example of someone who suffered from The Success Syndrome. We can now understand that he most probably suffered from success depression. According to one magazine report, "Within two years after his flight [to the moon], Buzz Aldrin checked into a psychiatric hospital on the verge of a nervous breakdown; he has since admitted he is a 'recovered alcoholic.' " This same report quotes a personal friend of Aldrin's who, in addition to noting this hero's current healthy status, added that Aldrin avoided talking to the press after his recovery "because he doesn't want to be exploited anymore."[5]

Although I have never met Aldrin or had access to his psychiatric case records, published reports of the problems he encountered after his moon walk and his ultimate illness conform to a pattern that is quite familiar to me: An individual climbs to the top of his profession with applied intelligence and diligence; success follows with its inevitable consequences—prestige, freedom, and power; at some point and in some context far removed from the original accomplishments, his reputation, status, or prestige *continues* to bring him the rewards of noncontingent success; success depression follows.

An earmark of all individuals subjected to noncontingent success (e.g., fashion models, "boss's sons"), and victims of success depression in particular, is that they come to *actively resent* the rewards, awards, praise, or kudos they receive in the absence of instrumental behavior. They feel "bought" or, as noted above in the Aldrin case, "exploited." The positive consequences of success, intended to reward and please, have a punitive effect when given to those who feel that they are being rewarded for who they are, *not* for what they are doing. In far too many cases resembling Aldrin's, the consequences of noncontingent success extend far beyond "bad feelings" of exploitation. Many ex-heroes and former greats end up requiring psychiatric care.

In summary, the experience of success leads to various types of losses—of actual rewards, of reinforcing interpersonal ties, or of control over reinforcers—and these losses are what account for the problem of success depression. Those who suffer from this severe disorder are unfortunately often denied sympathy, and may even experience criticism, for expressing their distress. Most of those who associate with success depressives assume that a person's successes would provide them with a source of pleasure, particularly if the rewards continued throughout the person's lifetime. The cruel paradox of success depression is that successes are often the root cause of the disease-producing losses.

The cry, "you have it all, why aren't you ecstatic?" cuts like a knife in the minds of achievers who know how many other types of reinforcers they've lost since the time they reached their sought-after goal. So too for ex-achievers who are provided with a variety of well-intentioned reinforcers that remind them they are no longer truly in control over their destinies as they once were "when they were great."

The losses that can result from success are many and often devastating. Yet, as we shall see in the next chapter, people are reluctant to abandon the pursuit of success or the reputation that they have "made it." In fact, the fear of losing the image and self-perception of being a success is often enough to drive one to drink.

## Chapter Nine

# "SELF-HANDICAPPING"

## Alcohol Abuse following Success

*"I'm alcoholic. . . . I thought only losers became alcoholics."*
> Jason Robards (from a National Council on
> Alcoholism advertisement)

Ex-stars and former greats are not the only ones who suffer as a result of noncontingent success experiences. As noted in our earlier analysis of the stress of success, personal beauty, ascribed status, connections with the "right" people, and so on, are often the sole determinants of the rewards an individual receives. Boss's sons (daughters, etc.) and other relatives of rich or powerful people, to name but one group, are frequently the recipients of a host of positive outcomes for *who* they are, not *what* they do. In those instances when an individual does not actually earn the reinforcers he receives—regardless of why—he will likely experience the disruptive effects of noncontingent success.

Geniuses are another group exposed to a unique variant of noncontingent success. Typically "discovered" as very young children, and singled out for an intellectual gift they have been born with, gifted children or child prodigies often receive far more praise—and considerably higher performance expectations—than they are equipped to handle.

The late Orson Welles was an individual who suffered from the burden of expectations well before his master-

155

work *Citizen Kane* hit the screen. Barbara Leaming, who
wrote a biography of Welles prior to his death, commented:

> Told that he was a prodigy for as long as he could
> remember, young Orson developed an air of confi-
> dence. . . . But for all his outward assurance, the child lived
> in constant fear of *not coming up to his parents' expectations:*
> "I always felt I was letting them down," he says now.
> "That's why I worked so hard. That's the stuff that turned
> the motor" [emphasis added].[1]

If we examine the effects of burdensome expectations derived from noncontingent success, we may get a better
understanding of why Welles felt so pressured to perform.
We may also gain insight as to why his tremendous promise remained unfulfilled throughout most of his "post-Kane"
life.

    When an individual's first (or most significant) ex-
posure to success is noncontingent, the result is often quite
devastating. The reason for this is typically unclear, since
the immediate *experience* of noncontingent success is fundamentally desirable. Virtually all but the insane or those
already wrecked by success long for the positive consequences of success that are offered recipients of noncontingent success. Yet the problem for these people is that
the *strings* and *expectations* attached to noncontingent success make it extremely threatening.

    The most deleterious consequence of noncontingent
success is its capacity to generate feelings of fear or ap-
prehension. Since noncontingent success is *not* derived
from instrumental behaviors, it leaves people wondering
what they did to deserve it, and how they will be able to
sustain top-level performances worthy of the feedback they

received. More important, noncontingent success experiences never provide an indication of what an individual must do to avoid losing the esteem gained by his specious success.

The recipient of noncontingent success is, thus, receiving fish with no knowledge of how to catch them. When people who do not know how to fish repeatedly receive fish from benefactors, they come to fear offending or "doing the wrong thing" *vis-à-vis* the benefactor and losing his largess. Their dependency upon outcomes that they did not bring about renders them helpless in influencing whether future rewards will continue without disruption, or end. In this regard they are like primitive *Homo sapiens*, making sacrifices to the gods of fertility. Neither understands the factors governing outcomes that he wishes to control, and they are both deathly afraid of losing rewards they experience as coming to them through luck, good fortune, or other reasons they can't quite comprehend.

In addition to suffering severe anxieties concerning their capacity to sustain their desired status, people who receive noncontingent success must also confront a knotty public relations dilemma. On the one hand, they must publicly live up to the expectatons implied by their success. This means *performing* in a manner that justifies their rewards. Consider, for example, a boss's son who for no other reason than his birthright is given control over a major division of a corporation. The prestige, power, and freedom that accompany managerial responsibility will be his despite the fact that were it not for the circumstances of his birth he might be working as a short-order cook. The problem awaiting him, however, is that along with the trappings of success go the responsibilities. This boss's son must manage his division of the corporation—

however he sees fit—or ultimately suffer the consequences. His task, and the task of others like him who
advance owing to noncontingent success experiences, is
far more difficult than that confronting the typical recipient
of an MBA.

On the other hand, recipients of noncontingent success want to *preserve* the positive outcomes given the successful. For the individual, uncertain as to how his noncontingent success came to be, and totally uncertain as to
whether or not he is capable of executing the instrumental
behaviors necessary to *deserve* or earn success, the safest
and most effective means available for preserving success
might be *not* performing.

The boss's son who is literally *given* a corporate division to manage must, at some point, determine how he
expects to retain *both* his self-esteem and the prestige, power,
and freedom that "come with the territory." Two options
present themselves. If he refuses the managerial position,
he can never be exposed as lacking managerial skill *and*
he can never derive the benefits of success. If he accepts
the job, he is handed success with the risk that he will be
exposed as being undeserving by evaluations of his on-
the-job performance. One of the more common, albeit ultimately maladaptive, resolutions of this dilemma is *"self-
handicapping"* behavior.[2]

Self-handicapping is a term that was coined to describe a variety of ostensibly *self-defeating* actions that, paradoxically, provide an individual with a means of *preserving* the status and favorable image of competence derived
from noncontingent success. In essence, self-handicapping is enacted when a person trying to protect his self-
esteem seeks out and appropriates impediments to success
or justifications for failure. Self-handicapping behaviors
accomplish a strategic goal: they interfere with a person's
ability to perform as well as he could have were it not for

the "handicap." This tactic enables the self-handicapper to obscure the meaning of subsequent evaluations. Despite the complex-sounding nature of this behavior pattern, its operations and effects are actually quite straightforward.

## SELF-HANDICAPPING WITH ALCOHOL

If you observe a dart-thrower scoring over 50% bull's-eyes, you would likely have a strong expectation that he could do it again a short time later. There is at least one activity, however, that would completely change your expectations regarding the dart-thrower's capacity to repeat his success: excessive alcohol consumption one-half hour *prior* to his throwing darts again.

Alcohol has a widespread reputation as a drug which temporarily disrupts coordination and concentration—the two attributes essential to skilled dart-throwing and most other behaviors that bring about success. Anyone who saw the successful dart-thrower drink three or four martinis after a 50% bull's-eye-level performance would *believe* that he could do it again if sober, but, given the fact that he is "under the influence" of alcohol, would *expect* the effects of this drug to disrupt his performance.

If you study this scenario carefully, it is apparent that drinking to excess following a successful performance can, paradoxically, provide a significanct *benefit* to the successful dart-thrower who may, for whatever reason, doubt his capacity to repeat successful performances. The most immediate benefit provided by this strategically timed alcohol abuse is the *preservation* of the image of competency. Consuming excessive amounts of alcohol buys him a time-limited reprieve; the validity of at least the next assessment is invalidated. By adopting a transient handicap known to impair performance capabilities, a successful individual can *temporarily* avoid fulfilling the performance expectations derived from prior successes. He is also in a position to avoid the implications of a failed performance while preserving the public and private assumption that were he not "under the influence," he would perform as expected.

An observer, who views a dart-thrower hitting 50% bull's-eyes *then* drinking excessively, would undoubtedly suspend any expectation that the dart-thrower could perform as before *until the effects of the alcohol had worn off.* In addition, and most important, this same observer would not assume any less inherent competence on the part of the dart-thrower were he to fail while drunk. Alcohol's effects do not wipe out ability, they merely suppress its manifestations. The successful dart-thrower, or any successful person for that matter, is afforded a "time-out" from demonstrating his abilities when under the transient influence of a drug such as alcohol. When the effects of drinking have worn off, the successful person has lost no status or stature insofar as his *presumed* abilities go, and is once again expected to prove his competence.

## WHY PEOPLE SELF-HANDICAP

It is safe to say that most dart-throwers capable of scoring rounds of 50% bull's-eyes will never be motivated, or feel a need, to self-handicap. There are, however, occasions when individuals "score" or are successful beyond their wildest imagination, and are then motivated to adopt self-protective, self-handicapping behaviors. These successes are sometimes a function of luck. Other times they may be a function of factors external to the performance setting altogether, as in being beautiful or being born into a family with excellent social connections. Regardless of how these noncontingent successes come about, the consequence for recipients of these coveted outcomes remains the same: They must either protect their image of competence in future situations involving assessments of their ability, or suffer the loss of the image of being a success. Thus, we see that self-handicapping is a disorder particular to individuals who have a shaky history of success and who are easily threatened by evaluations. Nevertheless, every self-handicapper has a history of success significant enough to have generated expectations that he can perform at a level deserving of success. With no image to protect, there exists no need to self-handicap. The purpose of self-handicapping is to *defend* a favorable but tenuous image of competency against the threats posed by periodic evaluations or assessments of ability.

I have concluded, based upon clinical data obtained from patients over the years, that all people who self-handicap *want* to believe that they are successful, but can't owing to their having experienced noncontingent successes in their lives: "Were they rewarding me for what I did or who I am?" By self-handicapping, the insecurity and doubt can be *temporarily* eliminated. In effect, the self-handicapper converts the internal doubt and insecurity he feels into external ambiguity, obfuscating his potentially substandard performances through behavior such as alcohol abuse. Should a self-handicapper who was previously the recipient of noncontingent success fail after overindulging in alcohol, he clouds the implications of his failure. Observers who would ordinarily wonder why he failed given the fact that he was once successful can conclude that it was due to *what he had to drink*, not *what he can do* (when sober and unencumbered).

It should be noted that self-handicapping theory is supported by experimental investigations demonstrating conclusively that experiences of noncontingent success throughout one's life can motivate self-protective alcohol abuse[3]. In a number of laboratories across the nation, this phenomenon has been replicated using an experimental paradigm that I developed in 1975. This research involves exposing experimental subjects to either success feedback (for taking a test containing questions that they can answer) or noncontingent success feedback (following a test with insoluble questions that they can only guess at), followed by a choice of (actually bogus) drugs or unlimited quantities of alcohol to consume prior to an anticipated retesting of their abilities.

Self-handicapping theory predicted that subjects who received contingent success feedback—who knew how and why they earned a good test score—would have no need to self-handicap by electing to receive a drug capable of impeding their performance. On the other hand, it was reasoned that subjects exposed to noncontingent success would feel quite differently after hearing that they had performed well on a test for which they had had to guess at the answers and would have to perform again. Thus, these individuals might feel that they were lucky, did not deserve success, would probably be "found out" on a retesting of their abilities, and need protection against being exposed as frauds upon retesting. Prior to the promised retesting, these subjects were expected to choose performance-inhibiting drugs (or consume excessive amounts of alcohol) as "protection" against failure. The experimental data other psychologists and I have gathered to date have provided conclusive support for this prediction.[4]

## SELF-HANDICAPPING DISORDERS

The preceding discussion presented self-handicapping behavior in its "classic" form: an intermittent, self-protective strategy, whereby an individual with a fear of losing esteem drinks excessively prior to an upcoming evaluation to avoid any implication of a possible failure. What is yet to be described is what I have seen in psychiatric hospitals and in my private clinical practice: self-handicapping as a full-blown psychiatric disorder that is not limited to transient self-protective acts. Regrettably, many people become "career" self-handicappers.

Intermittent, nonaddictive alcohol abuse is the most widely recognized method for enacting self-handicapping strategies.[5] The prototype of a *career* self-handicapper is an *alcoholic* who began his "drinking" following a professional life marked by early successes, lucky breaks, or "super scores" so spectacular that he thought they could never be equaled, let alone surpassed. Nevertheless, *any* symptom that can account for why an individual fails to perform as expected (on the job, in school, or even in the bedroom) qualifies as a self-handicapping "agent." I have personally treated patients who have self-handicapped using chronic procrastination, depression, and panic attacks to justify failure in anticipation of performance evaluations. Some of my colleagues have noted that a host of other disorders, including obesity, asthma, and grief reactions, can function temporarily to account for why a recipient of noncontingent success would fail to live up to performance expectations.

The danger inherent in every instance when an individual uses a symptom to blur the implications of evaluations is that its use may become chronic. Every one of us has used symptoms such as occasional alcohol abuse, bad moods, or periodic procrastination to preemptively prepare for potential failure in important interactions. The most common context for this is prior to important business meetings or examinations of ability: "Gee, Harry, I doubt that I'll be myself today at the board meeting considering the fact that I didn't sleep last night and my head *continues* to throb from all that wine."

Most students who, in their anxiety, put off studying for an exam or preparing a term paper find relief in proclaiming, prior to receipt of their grades, "I probably didn't perform up to par on this test; I had no time to study." Such behavior, exhibited on occasion, is normal and is a universally accepted defense against the performance anxiety inherent in any important evaluation. However, when every meeting or examination is preempted by such symptoms as nights on the town, "one too many drinks," counting sheep until the alarm rings, or psychosomatic ailments, a psychiatric disorder is present.[6]

The road from self-handicapping alcohol abuse—the self-protective strategy—to alcoholism—the psychiatric disorder—is a simple, sad, and direct one. To begin with, some of the people who initiate alcohol abuse as an intermittent self-handicapping strategy can become physically addicted to alcohol as one might become addicted to the nicotine in cigarettes. Others become addicted to the relief from anxiety afforded by self-handicapping.

Recall that the self-handicapper initiates alcohol abuse as a means of relieving the anxiety derived from fears of losing the esteem gained from noncontingent success. If self-handicapping behavior works, and it typically does at first, it reinforces a person by *both* relieving the anxiety of anticipated performances and protecting the image of competency he has acquired. Prior to a test of the abilities of the drunk self-handicapper, he can say, "I have nothing to fear from this impending evaluation—I can blame a failure on the booze. If I succeed *in spite of my handicap,* I'll look like a superman for having succeeded under less than optimal conditions." The fact that drinking alcohol can induce such thoughts and feelings makes it reinforcing, and likely to be repeated over and over again.

Once self-handicapping alcohol abuse becomes the rule and *not* the occasional exception, it ceases to protect an individual's self-esteem. The more the recipient of noncontingent success gains relief and protection via alcohol abuse, the less likely he will be to report sober for a legitimate observation of his abilities. As fears of being exposed as undeserving of success reach extreme heights, all incentives to determine whether or not one does in fact have the abilities necessary to earn success vanish. The more an anxious person turns to alcohol, the more he will come to fear the diagnostic test which could free him from his burgeoning dependency. In a short time, a full-blown alcohol dependence disorder can develop from this pattern of avoidant behavior. Thus, what started as a means of obtaining transient relief has become a full-fledged disease. A case history of an individual who drank only after he had become a success, and nearly destroyed his life with what began as self-handicapping alcohol abuse following noncontingent success, is presented in Chapter 11.

## Chapter Ten

# FEAR OF SUCCESS

## Self-Destructing When "The Top" Is in Sight

*So much the more surprising, indeed bewildering, must it appear when as a physician one makes the discovery that people occasionally fall ill precisely because a deeply-rooted and long cherished wish has come to fulfillment.*

Sigmund Freud

All of the success-induced disorders examined thus far have one aspect in common: they occur in successful people who *fear the loss* of tangible rewards that they have acquired, or a prestigious position that exists or once existed. Underachievers and status inconsistents fear the loss of their respective social networks, a dominant source of reinforcement in day-to-day living. Those who experience "where do I go from here?" depressions suffer the loss of simple pleasures enjoyed previous to success or a loss of control over the reinforcers currently in their lives. Self-handicappers are the most fearful group of all. Being uncertain as to precisely why they are successful and how they can sustain the stature they derive from success, they are ever vigilant to defend against evaluations that can strip them of their "riches."

In contrast to others who are "wrecked by success"—as Freud called victims of what we now call The Success Syndrome—the men and women who suffer from a *fear of success* are unique. Although these people *do* have ample reason to believe that they are capable of producing quality performances guaranteed to result in successful outcomes, their disorder prevents them from achieving their goals the moment success appears to be in hand. Individuals with "classic" cases of a fear of success, not some variant of the disorders discussed above, fail to live up to their potential or realize their ambitions while suffering this disorder. Their symptoms literally block them from behaving in a manner that would enable them to reach their goals.

The distinguishing feature of people who fear success is the intense anxiety they suffer from *anticipating* the consequences of success. Unlike the underachiever who actually hears his peers taunt "bookworm," or the self-handicapper who knows that he had a leg up on the competition because his girlfriend's father was the judge of the contest, the "success-fearer" typically does not have a justification based in "reality" for the anxiety that sabotages his pursuit of success.

Psychiatric research has concluded that the person who fears success suffers from unconscious guilt.[1] There is a consensus in the field that the unconscious guilt preventing these people from succeeding dates back to infantile sexual conflicts or what is commonly called the Oedipus complex. Psychoanalyst Otto Fenichel maintains that for those who fear success, "success may mean the achievement of something unmerited or wrong."[2] Specifically, "wrong" in this context refers to a child's success in the Oedipal struggle.

The Oedipus complex or Oedipal stage of development, occurring in early childhood roughly between the ages of 3 and 6, marks a time when a child exhibits an unconscious tendency to become greatly attached to the parent of the opposite sex and feels hostile, envious, and aggressive toward the parent of the same sex. Several intense conflicts arise from this attachment. To begin with, wanting one parent exclusively and feeling aggressively toward the other deprives the child of contact with the same-sex parent. More important, the aggressiveness felt toward the parent of the same sex arouses the fear that this parent will retaliate against the child for his feelings. This fear of retaliation, dubbed "castration anxiety" by psychoanalysts who focused primarily upon the male child's fears of retaliation, is in fact a global fear of the consequences of a child of either sex stepping into, and filling the shoes of, the parent of the same sex.

The successful resolution of the conflicts inherent in this developmental period involves establishing a positive identification with the parent of the same sex. This bonding is dubbed "identification with the aggressor," since it is presumed that the child experiencing Oedipal hostilities toward the parent of the same sex projects comparable levels of aggressiveness onto that parent. When successful, this identification typically results in healthy strivings and attitudes toward achieving success. Instead of sustaining conflict with the parent of the same sex who is presumed to be more powerful and is capable of retaliation, the child adopts an "if you can't beat 'em join 'em attitude" that permits him (her) to go off on his own and strive to be as powerful as daddy (mommy).

For many individuals, however, the Oedipus complex is not resolved successfully. For some reason, the child does not form a healthy identification with the parent of the same sex, fails to abandon his longing for attachment to the parent of the opposite sex, or comes to believe that his hostile, envious, or aggressive feelings may achieve their intended aim. This lack of resolution, called a "fixation" owing to the fact that the child's psychological evolution is arrested or "fixated" at this developmental stage, is frequently the point of origin for the guilt that successfearers experience throughout their lives.

The reasons why an individual would fail to adequately resolve his Oedipal conflicts are virtually limitless.

There exists a consensus within the psychiatric community which maintains that factors such as having parents who are either too ineffectual to challenge (in terms of authority, disciplinary control, and so on), or too bullying and hostile to identify with, may preclude a resolution of Oedipal conflicts. When the parent of the same sex is so weak and ineffectual that even the child's anger proves to distress him, the child feels inordinate guilt over his strength and dominance. Conversely, if the parent of the same sex is too dominant a force, the child's anger will be the source of terrific anxiety since it might trigger a murderous response on the part of that parent. Other factors accounting for fixations during this period of development include parents whose interactive styles are very inconsistent, intense sibling rivalries that involve aggressive and/or assertive impulses, or excessive pressures on the child to assume the role of the parent of the same sex before that child has had an opportunity to develop an adequate sense of self.

## FEELINGS OF OEDIPAL GUILT IN ONE'S ADULT LIFE

The dominant thrust of the psychoanalytic or Freudian interpretation of the fear of success phenomenon focuses on those who have failed to resolve their Oedipal conflicts. It is assumed that for these individuals, success in adult life can revive repressed anxieties deriving from childhood yearnings to succeed against the parent of the same sex for the attention and affection of the parent of the opposite sex. More to the point, individuals who have Oedipal fixations commonly carry with them childhood *fears of retaliation* by the parent of the same sex should they *ever* be successful in achieving their goals.

For the child who has not resolved his Oedipal conflicts, an opportunity to succeed in later life may evoke the unconscious fear that if he succeeds he will fall victim to his parent's retaliation. Success or goal-attainment now assumes a positive and a negative valence. Winning, for the individual with an Oedipal fixation, also means losing. Since this individual's conflicts regarding success are deeply rooted in his subconscious, he is typically totally unaware of why he cannot grasp success when it is at hand; he knows only that he is afraid to do so and sabotages his efforts before they subject him to a fate that for him is subconsciously equivalent to risking death.

*A Word about Autonomy.* Many psychoanalytic theorists assert that in addition to Oedipal fixations, a major source of fears of success are parent–child interactions that focus on the child's autonomy or independence. Simply stated, all children must, at some point in their development, see themselves as becoming separate and independent of their parents in order for them to develop a healthy sense of self-esteem. The child who cannot give up his dependence upon his parents to express his own feelings and enact goal-directed behaviors of his own choosing will, in a word, become sick.

Frequently it is not the child who fails to attempt a separation from his parents but, instead, it is the parents who hold the child back from asserting himself and making his own decisions. Owing to their own insecurities and neuroses, some parents view a child's natural self-expression of autonomy as a rejection of their role in his life and view his independent behaviors as competitive with their desires. They convey these negative feelings to the child in various ways, ranging from overt expressions of anger to subtle threats of abandonment.

The result of these parental sanctions against the child's striving for self-defined goals is that desires for autonomy become fused with feelings of anxiety. Since a child who has controlling parents comes to expect that he will be abandoned, deprived of parental love, or punished for his attempts to become independent, he is likely to learn how to suppress desires for, and behaviors in pursuit of, autonomy.

A child who is punished—either explicitly or implicitly—for striving toward independence will fear successful achievements throughout his life owing to the fact that they are adult manifestations of autonomy. Because this child learned at a very early age to suppress fundamental strivings for achievement, he will have lost the capacity to define what kinds of self-assertiveness or self-expression can be tolerated and what kinds will reliably be punished. This "overgeneralized" control or subconscious prohibition against any expressions of autonomy is what prevents the success-fearer from demonstrating his abilities and securing goals that are at hand.

## SYMPTOMS MANIFESTED BY THOSE WHO FEAR SUCCESS

The preceding discussion of a fear of success presents a much stricter definition of the disorder than is found in many psychoanalytic writings.[3] Many authors fail to discriminate among the variety of self-sabotaging or aversive reactions that people can have in anticipation, or as a consequence, of success. In our analysis of The Success Syndrome, however, fear of success refers only to disorders that occur *in anticipation of succeeding.*

The person who fears success has a variety of mechanisms at his disposal that can successfully block his climb up the ladder of success. It is not so much *what* the success-fearer does to him- or herself, but *when* it is done that demonstrates his or her subconscious, self-sabotaging intent. As Freud noted, success-fearers "fall ill" precisely because a longed-for goal is *about to be* realized. This may be through any one of a number of incapacitating diseases or disorders, as long as they guarantee that the goal will not be attained.

A more subtle version of this strategy involves alienating people who are important to an overall goal or are actually the goal itself. Many success-fearing businesspeople will alienate supervisors, important co-workers, or customers, in anticipation of promotions or receipt of greater responsibility. However, when this tactic fails to achieve its intended self-sabotaging goal, the person who fears success will often simplify the process by internalizing the alienation, and feel it toward his job, the firm, or the entire industry, and quit.

Often, another person is the only goal someone is striving to attain. For the success-fearer with a severe Oedipal fixation, the prospect of marriage can evoke an inordinate amount of guilt. In cases such as this, a fear of success is often manifested through a variety of sexual symptoms. A male with intense Oedipal guilt and a fear of succeeding with women (who symbolize his mother) will often suffer manifestations of sexual impotence such as premature ejaculation or a failure to achieve erection with a "marriageable" partner. This mode of "passive failure" sabotages the possibility of marriage for the success-fearer—a success that would evoke terrible guilt and anxiety. Yet he can still maintain the conscious illusion that he is actually otherwise healthy and desirous of mature relationships with women; it is only his impotence, he reasons, that stands in his way.

Conversely, those men who fear "successful" relationships with women who would make appropriate spouses may alternatively become sexually promiscuous or "Don Juans"; they thus fail to find happiness or satisfaction with any woman who appears capable of providing them with a gratifying relationship. In this case, dissatisfaction with the woman is expressed in a symptomatic form—sexually. Promiscuity—an *overinvolvement* with women—disguises the underlying anxiety of succeeding in a relationship with one woman. Such a relationship, for an individual with an unresolved Oedipal conflict, would evoke castration anxiety.[4]

In a manner that closely parallels self-handicapping behavior, the symptoms evoked by a fear of success typically prevent a person from achieving success by inhibiting his or her goal-oriented pursuits. Other times a fear of success requires an individual to drop out of the race altogether. The underemployed genius is the most common example of this phenomenon. By simply setting his level of aspiration so far below that that would represent a success according to his value system, this person avoids suffering the anticipated aversive consequences of being successful. He presents his desires to the world as though he were a high-IQ Porgy: "Nothin' of a career's plenty for me." I have treated two individuals who represent such classic illustrations of this kind of behavior that their cases warrant a brief discussion.

The first was a 43-year-old single man who worked at a medical library checking out books, not as a librarian. He functioned at one of the lowest rungs on the hierarchical ladder of the library staff. He also had an IQ hovering near 155 (110 is average; 145 is the minimum standard for genius). This man was the second of two sons born to a prominent attorney who ruled his household in a tyrannical manner. Another interesting point is that the patient's brother, whom he idealized, committed suicide when the patient was a collegiate honor's student on the dean's list.

From the initial stages of therapy, it was apparent to me that not only was he unable to work through his Oedipal struggle with his father, but some of his childhood guilt caused him to feel responsibility for his brother's suicide. It was as though the patient saw his brother as suffering death for his achievements in college, which, according to the patient's twisted rationale, should have brought punishment on *him*.

Following the trauma of his brother's suicide, and prior to his senior year of college assured of summa cum laude, the patient withdrew from active competition for grades, academic honors, and career goals. Instead, he dropped out of college and busied himself with readings in philosophy and psychiatry, attempting to find an understanding of, in his words, "this shitpile called life." He tried two religions and at least six psychotherapists. Finally, we started working together and thankfully were somewhat successful. He was able, for the first time in his life, to accept that his job and general withdrawal from competitive pursuits were symptomatic of his need to avoid achieving at all costs. Once he identified the source of his problems, he pursued and obtained a bachelor's degree. He is no longer working at the circulation desk of the library, but is still dissatisfied, and functioning in a vocation far beneath his abilities and true desires.

The second case was a 28-year-old single woman, employed as a secretary by a female department head at a prestigious New England college. This woman had dropped out of another prestigious school with an outstanding reputation for its liberal arts programs, though she only had slightly more than one semester's work remaining for her bachelor's degree. Prior to dropping out, she had made the dean's list every semester. Her reason for leaving school and moving to Boston was to escape a relationship with a possessive, demanding boyfriend, who was given to jealous rages.

She arrived in Boston at the age of 20 and took a secretarial position ostensibly to earn extra money prior to returning to school the following year. Despite this intention, she has remained a secretary unable or unwilling to complete her schooling at any of the Boston-area colleges, even through night courses. Instead, she works for a woman who is clearly not her intellectual equal, serving this woman's every need. She has also been unable to engage in a gratifying relationship with a male. All of her suitors have, in some fashion, either abused or failed to appreciate her.

This patient suffered from an extremely conflictual Oedipal period. She was an unplanned child, born to a mother who was 36 and not desirous of a fourth child. On the other hand, the patient's father was overjoyed at her birth; his first three children had been boys. The patient grew up as the most adored object in her father's life, easily surpassing her mother's place in the eyes of her father. Moreover, she was pampered and spoiled by her brothers. Despite the fact that she supplanted the mother's position in the family along several dimensions, her mother never manifested overt hostility. Instead, she often joked about leaving, so the patient could "have the boys all to [herself]."

This brief review of the overeducated secretary's plight indicates how children who "*win*" Oedipal conflicts ultimately lose, by punishing themselves throughout their life for victories they perceive as "wrong." It was never this patient's conscious intention to displace her mother from the role she deserved in the family; it just happened that her father and brothers all adored their "baby girl." Regrettably, this adoration, coupled with her mother's threatened abandonment, left the patient with a lifetime of guilt.

The patient has continued to atone for this guilt by failing to succeed in any sphere of her life, by remaining underemployed, and by partaking in relationships with men who undervalue her while she casts appreciative suitors aside.

Dr. Matina Horner has published research findings that have catapulted this phenomenon of success-fearing women to the public's attention.[5] Horner's research is important for a variety of reasons. It was the first statement of the contention that fear of success is as central to the lives of women as men. Recall that the terminology (e.g., castration anxiety), and case studies of fear-of-success phenomena reported by psychoanalysts, had for some time been predominantly male. Of greater significance to the study of fear-of-success disorders was Horner's demonstration of a cultural bias operating against women who strive for success. Horner argued that women were subjected to societal norms that punished assertive behavior on the part of women from childhood onward. This, coupled with the requirement to repress aggression during the Oedipal period, resulted in women being far less willing to seek success, and thereby settling for subordinate roles in society.

With our ever-changing attitudes toward female assertiveness, it is to be expected that future research findings will differ significantly from those obtained by Dr. Horner in 1968. What will not change, however, is the fact that anxiety and guilt derived from unresolved Oedipal conflicts will continue to cause countless numbers of competent and creative people to sabotage their abilities and fail to achieve success. Men and women alike, who fear retribution for success or believe that prior success was "wrongly" conferred on them, will fall ill or sabotage themselves in anticipation of adult success; that is, unless their subconscious conflicts are resolved.

★ ★ ★

The four preceding chapters have presented descriptions of the more common disorders deriving from success or the anticipation of it. They are by no means exhaustive in documenting every aversive reaction to The Success Syndrome, since such an undertaking would not be possible. Self-handicapping strategies and fear of success, to name but two disorders, can manifest themselves in innumerable ways.

Crucial to an understanding of The Success Syndrome is the need to evaluate when and how a successful—or potentially successful—person's symptoms become manifested. An executive who turns down a promotion that involves relocating to Chicago after having lived in a Florida seacoast town for most of his life does *not* necessarily have a disorder. However, a "status inconsistent" who fears social isolation and loss of peer group camaraderie as the result of a promotion might very well have a disorder. In a similar vein, it would be totally unwarranted to assume that every intelligent female secretary fears success. To understand a person's career and interpersonal choices, each case must be examined individually to determine if the behavior under observation is a consequence of some form of unhealthy anxiety or a rational, health-promoting decision.

Many people with no success-based problems would refuse to live in a big city for wholly rational reasons. Similarly, in the 1980s it is not uncommon to find executive secretaries who have status, high salaries, and freedom, and who are, in a word, successes! However, we now know that "a few drinks with the boys before the meeting," as well as sleepiness, migraine headaches, and quarrels, can all function as self-handicapping strategies depending upon when they occur. If the nature of a person's success and the timing of his symptoms follow a particular pattern, a determination of their meaning and his feelings about success is easily understood. To further illustrate the range of adverse reactions that occur in response to, and in anticipation of, success, I will, in the following section, present descriptions of individuals who have a personal awareness of how major life changes, nearly suicidal distress, and business reversals were all consequences of The Success Syndrome.

# PERSONAL ACCOUNTS OF THE SUCCESS SYNDROME

*Success is counted sweetest by those who ne'er succeed.*
Emily Dickinson

The sister sciences of psychiatry and psychology are often maligned for concentrating on "sick" or aberrant forms of human behavior. It is often assumed that since mental health professionals use their patients as the data base from which to derive theories of human functioning, they must be insensitive to the factors affecting the majority of people who adapt to the stresses and strains of everyday life. An implicit extension of this critique argues that mental illnesses are distinct from "normal" human functioning and, as such, have little bearing on how the bulk of mankind, without psychiatric disorders, function.

Most psychiatrists and psychologists are quick to counter this argument by indicating that many of the mental disorders they study and treat represent exaggerations of normal human functioning and are not distinct phenomena. We can most easily see this in the case of phobic disorders, which are, simply stated, fears of things, people, or places.

Although it is undeniably true that psychiatric disorders such as agoraphobia (a pathological fear and avoidance of open places, typically causing a patient to remain housebound) are not equivalent to the widespread fear of snakes, both phobic reactions share a set of common features. Snake phobics and agoraphobics both avoid certain stimuli, both experience distress when confronted with avoided stimuli, and both harbor irrational thoughts concerning the likelihood of encountering feared stimuli as well as the consequences of such encounters. In fact, all phobias are comprised of these component features. Distinctions among different phobias are determined by the phobic object, level of debilitation it causes, and the extent to which fears generalize across similar stimuli and situations.

Our analysis of The Success Syndrome has proceeded in a similar fashion. We have demonstrated that adverse reactions to success—both normal and pathological—occur along a continuum and differ *only* in terms of the degree of reaction, not in terms of the "kind" of response. For example, in our analysis of self-handicapping behavior, we noted that everyone can be expected to use external impediments to success (such as alcohol, situational demands, physical symptoms) as preemptive justifications for potential failure prior to important, anxiety-provoking evaluations. Yet only those with extreme anxieties concerning their capacity to perform as expected would resort to self-handicapping alcohol abuse with debilitating regularity.

In a similar vein, almost everyone accepts the contention that "it is lonely at the top," realizing that it is hard to relate to friends from the farm once you've lived in and enjoyed "Paree." Nevertheless, the vast majority of qualified individuals offered promotions that involve relocations or separation from familiar peer groups jump at the opportunity to advance their careers. A healthy person, with normal anxieties about social isolation and loneliness stemming from success, assumes that these aversive conditions will be transient and that his distress will end when he becomes integrated within a new community.

The primary focus of this chapter is on the thoughts of two acquaintances of mine who have experienced success as well as some of the problems it can cause. One interview is with a self-handicapper who was once the highest paid athlete in the world. The other is with a TV sportscaster who has first-hand knowledge of the distress, and strains in interpersonal relationships, that can result from achieving a much-sought-after goal.

Of the two individuals, only one, the self-handicapper, has suffered a psychiatric disorder. The other exemplifies a healthy individual who, though enjoying many benefits of success, has been adversely affected by the negative consequences of success. We should emphasize, however, that the "healthy victim" of The Success Syndrome did not have his life derailed by the distress he suffered; it only dampened the joy he had anticipated from his achievements. Otherwise, this individual functioned well in all phases of his life despite his experience of periodic distress.

Most of those who are, or once were, "wrecked by success" suffer only temporarily and ultimately continue a fully rewarding life. This point is not intended to minimize the fact that psychiatric disorders such as the ones described below can and have resulted from success. We should recognize that The Success Syndrome leads to a range of negative effects—some merely painful, others pathological. But all these problems affect successful people who would never be expected to suffer a psychiatric disorder were it not for the consequences of their success.

## THE APPLE CREEK KID

On July 31, 1985, the front page of *The Boston Herald* featured a picture of Mr. Bob Lobel and the accompanying headline: "He's 4 staying in Boston." The "4" has a double

meaning, referring both to Lobel's career orientation and
to the television station he works for. His decision not to
leave TV-4 prompted much attention from most media
sources around the Boston area. *The Boston Globe,* the city's
other daily, covered the story in detail. Local radio stations
included it as part of their newscasts, and some did live
interviews with the star. You see, in Boston and the greater
New England area, Bob Lobel is a celebrity's celebrity.

Bob Lobel had given up the chance to become nationally known. Had he been so inclined, he could have left
town in style with an offer from CBS-TV. But staying was
no hardship since he was given a purported five-year, $2.5
million contract, which makes Lobel one of the highest
paid sportscasters (actually, Sports Director of NBC's Boston affiliate, WBZ-TV) in the nation. However, the reason
why Bob decided to stay "local" in Boston, turning down
the CBS offer that would have given him national recognition and the potential for even greater success, had a
great deal to do with his first tastes of success and its
attendant "benefits."

Before examining the ways in which Lobel had felt
the stress of success, I should point out that he *earned* his
way to the top of his profession and millionaire status. He
has held several positions in both radio and television
sportscasting, and has earned three Emmy awards among
many accolades. Being the modest man that he is, however, Lobel is reluctant to attribute his success to an ov-
erabundance of insight into TV journalism or great skill at
writing stories. He is, however, quick to admit that he has
learned to develop a rapport with whatever type of person
he meets. In fact, he acknowledges that one of the keys
to his current success and enormous popularity is the sense
of personal intimacy he generates in his audience.

This capacity to engage the affection of people is something that did not come naturally to Bob. It must truly be seen as a skill in much the same sense that throwing darts or writing legal briefs involves abilities that must be practiced constantly and honed to be perfected. In Bob's case, his capacity to get along extremely well with people is undoubtedly a consequence of the difficult adjustments he was forced to make as a child. It is safe to assume that at least part of Bob's "empathic" ability developed as a result of his having to move to a variety of new residences, forcing him to earn the affection of new schoolmates:

> I'm an only child who grew up in Apple Creek, Ohio. Actually, my parents moved a couple of times when I was a kid. When I was 11, in the 6th grade, I absolutely didn't want to move . . . it was awful for me—actually traumatic. I had to start school late, in the middle of the year, and I had no friends and school was the most horribly lonely and painful place you could imagine. Well, I excelled at sports and wanted to be accepted, so I did both. I had this drive to succeed—being liked and a jock—and I ended up as co-captain of our championship football team when I was in high school. . . . I was actually always shy and bashful, but by combining my athletic drive and my authentic affection for people, I learned that I could succeed. As I grew to learn to be comfortable in particular settings [i.e., sports], I knew I could get along fantastically with people.

And "get along" he did and continues to do. The "market share" ratings that his sportscasts receive are the actual reason why Boston's NBC affiliate was willing to make Bob a millionaire. A less tangible indicator of his popularity from the TV station's perspective, but one that Bob cherishes, are the fan's reactions when he is in public. I've been with him several times when he was preparing stories or watching sporting events, and can say that the amount of recognition he attracts is staggering. It is also the "fuel" that is in large measure responsible for his apparent love of his job.

> I know that I really work well with people in crowds . . . I get energy from them. I mean I can walk into the Boston Garden [home of the Celtics and Bruins] and just feel it. It's actually one of the most important parts of the job for me. . . . Like a good politician who cares about his constituents, I couldn't be doing my job as it should be done if I didn't have an honest rapport and a genuine desire to relate to people.

But the very fact that Bob is a celebrity has, at times, threatened his capacity to "relate" to people. The jock who worked his way to the top of Boston television by being able to communicate well with people was being warped by his success. In a very real sense, Bob's popularity once threatened his ability to sustain his success.

> I still deliver the sports, but I am now a celebrity and a "personality" and being in that role is not only a burden, it takes a lot of time and energy to do all that people expect of you. I know the reason I'm getting the amount of money that I do is because I'm a celebrity, but I resent it. *Actually,* [my celebrity status] *is starting to hamper my work.* I have always been a "people person." I work well in groups . . . I actually get energy from crowds. But now, I'm sensing that people are developing a fear of approaching me. I feel that I have to cut down the range of my emotional expression because what I feel is no longer just an emotion, it's a "star" emotion, and it gets amplified all out of proportion. A bit of anger and people say I'm a raging prima donna; a bit of pride in my work, and someone calls it egomania. It's not the way I am or want to be. I'm feeling terribly squeezed

by this public awareness of my moods . . . it's making me watch myself and become much more guarded than I like.

The burdens of success and stardom have also affected Bob Lobel's personal life. This people-oriented jock and college fraternity president now finds himself quite cautious about forming and opening himself up in new friendships. In essence, the shyness that motivated Bob to express himself through sports and to develop interpersonal relationships when he was younger is reemerging as a consequence of his success:

> Celebrity status is like a double-edged sword when it comes to friendships. You are permitted, owing to the vast number of social contacts you have, to make a lot of new friends on a superficial level, but very very few friends at an intimate level. You're forced to evaluate people a lot closer, whereas in high school or college there was never a thought of evaluating your friends . . . you either liked them or you didn't. Now, you introspect and ask, "Hey, is this guy genuine, is he after something?" I find that I have this basic level of concern that I feel comes from questioning whether people want to be my friend because I have something that they want because of who I am or what I am. I'm really just trying to protect the quality of my relationships with people.

The preceding remarks should bring to mind the painful lament of Tennessee Williams, who called his success a "kind of death," and grew inordinately distrustful—virtually paranoid—of friends, whom he suspected of manipulative or false praise. Regrettably, this dilemma is quite common among the successful. A recent *Vanity Fair* cover story about Maria Shriver, entitled "Growing Up Kennedy," began with the following lead-in: "The labels are inevitable: Sargent Shriver's daughter, J.F.K.'s niece, CBS anchorwoman. . . . But behind it all . . . Maria Shriver is a highly motivated woman who's coped with growing up Kennedy."[1] According to Ms. Shriver, this sort of "introduction" really upsets her:

> All those commas—the daughter of, the girlfriend of, the granddaughter of, the niece of—I hate them! What absolutely drives me is to be considered as somebody outside the commas, somebody considered for her work alone. . . . What do people exactly want from me? Do they want me for my work or because of who my family is?[2]

Although Shriver's pedigree has done nothing to derail her quest for success, comparably "noble" ancestry has been implicated in the death of one of her cousins (David Kennedy), and the suffering encountered by countless Kennedys, boss's sons, and others who have achieved significant degrees of public recognition. In fact, next to depressions born of excessive performance expectations, the most commonly occurring symptom that I have noted among successful people or their children is the depression derived from not being able to determine if the love they receive is authentically for them or attributable to their status.

In addition to the problems of interpersonal trust that he encounters, Bob Lobel's experience of The Success Syndrome extends to his sense of personal well-being. Despite working long and hard to achieve his goals, he found that his first taste of success did not provide the "internal feeling" of satisfaction that he anticipated. With success and its positive consequences—prestige, freedom, and power— Bob noticed a change within himself that was not at all comforting. As he tells it, he now gets so many rewards just for being *who he is*, he has come to think of himself in terms appropriate to the Oriental man *given* a fish, not taught to fish:

> What has happened to me as a result of all this success is that I've become a "consumer" not a "producer." Before I was always building something, creating a new project or concept. Now, I'm growing fat, literally and figuratively. I find I'm just holding on and holding off people with either excessive expectations or petty jealousies. . . . You see, I enjoy expending the most energy to achieve new heights, that's where the most fulfillment is derived. After I have achieved something, doing it again is never as much fun or as rewarding. Subsequent rewards are just handed to you. For me, once you actually achieve something it's like giving up something. It's giving up the motivation to achieve, which in itself is a major loss.

Like so many successful people who begin to over-analyze themselves for weaknesses once they reach the top, Lobel has known the fear of loss that results from achieving.

> Sure I had some fears when I considered going to [CBS-TV in New York]. They didn't really know me like folks [in Boston] do, and I feared that they might find something about me that they didn't like once I got there. I also feared that maybe I was just really lucky here, that I wasn't really good or worthy of my success. Worst of all, what if I started losing my ability to communicate, the charisma, whatever magic I had that kept the audience tuned? When you're at the top, you can always start slipping down the other side. At some point you just can't keep on achieving more and more success; it seems like failure is the only thing left.

Bob's concern that failure was the only thing left is, to any rational observer, a fear symptomatic of The Success

Syndrome. His current contract with WBZ-TV in Boston is for five years, and makes him a millionaire. But it does far more than that for the Apple Creek Kid; it insulates him from the aversive consequences of The Success Syndrome.

Bob's contract with WBZ-TV contains all the elements necessary to ensure that his success will never become excessively burdensome or disease-provoking. It provides him with new responsibilities that are *challenging* (to evoke eustress), not threatening, and does nothing to further isolate this "people person" from the fans who fuel his creative drive. In fact, Bob told me that all of his future projects would enhance his contact with audiences rather than isolate him in a distant, executive role. Most important, Bob's employers convincingly assured him that they were investing in his future as a person, and were confident that his personality and talent were responsible for his high ratings. When an individual feels authentic pride and, more important, sincere affection from others—be it one's employers or one's audience—it is not possible to be permanently victimized by The Success Syndrome.

When Bob and I had a chance to meet within a week of his headline-making contract signing, he had this to say about the biggest success of his life:

> How does it feel? I'm honestly relieved that it's over. I knew I was going to come out of [the negotiations] pretty well, with a good deal no matter what I did. But I also always knew that the money and the material things were never the issues. It was peace of mind and personal satisfaction. I'm overjoyed to know where my career will be going; to feel challenged again. I have more options, more freedom, and new responsibilities. But more than what the station has given me in terms of new projects to conquer, they demonstrated to me [with their contract offer] that

they really do appreciate me and want me both for who I am and for what I've done.

In his own words, Bob told me he had achieved his success through hard work, and was able to find joy in rewards he knew he deserved. He had earned his positive sense of self-esteem the only way possible: by doing what he could do best and having his behavior reinforced by employers and fans. Despite suffering intermittent anxiety and self-doubt, and experiencing some difficulties interacting with people after achieving his success, Bob did not succumb to the serious disorders that can develop from The Success Syndrome, owing to a considerable sense of self-esteem. It is virtually certain that all future successes will bring Bob nothing but satisfaction and joy.

## ACCOUNTING FOR "EXTREME" SUCCESSES

"Why did this happen to me?" is a lament most commonly associated with individuals subjected to catastrophes. The biblical Job is the prototypic "innocent" victim of the punitive acts of God. Job knew he had been good and felt he had suffered God's wrath without cause. As a consequence, he cried heavenward, pleading for an explanation.

Most people would want a life in stark contrast to Job's; one wherein God showers them with *good fortune* and riches, not curses. We seek to arrange our lives in such a way as to never look a "gift horse" in the mouth; few people ask "why" when the outcome is favorable. If you ask for a contract paying $600,000 for three years and are given a salary of $600,000 *per* year, shut up, and enjoy!

The problem, as we have seen, is that it is often impossible to "enjoy" an inordinately favorable outcome you cannot understand or explain. Striking it rich can turn relatively normal, contented people into anxious suffering Jobs if their windfalls were obtained when they were *not* prospecting for gold.

Noncontingent successes evoke their own particular brand of "why did this happen to me" inquiries. Their purpose, in contrast to Job's queries, which sought an explanation for his horrible fate, is intended to identify what warranted an extremely *favorable* outcome. While Job searched in vain for the faults or sins that would have justified his suffering, the victim of noncontingent success searches for the virtues, abilities, or positive traits that could account for the blessings he received.

The reason why Job and recipients of noncontingent success search for explanations is really quite simple. Psychologists have demonstrated, in a variety of ways, that humans have an innate tendency to believe in a just world. People assume that good things happen to good people, and that if you are bad, your fortunes will follow suit. There is a part of the socialized human psyche that leads us to believe, "Ye shall reap what ye shall sow."[3] Thus, because of this "innate" belief system, people reflexively respond to very intense or extreme outcomes—either positive *or* negative—by questioning what they did to deserve what happened.

An inherent danger in such questioning is that often, as Job discovered, one can find no adequate answer. Some outcomes must be viewed as capricious, or unexplainable acts of God, since there are no rational explanations for their occurrence. This is ultimately accepted by most people following disasters, since the history of mankind is replete with instances of bad things happening to good people. Isn't it said that "the good die young"?

A special dilemma exists when noncontingent *successes* are the outcomes that need explaining. On the one hand, our culture makes it very difficult to accept unearned success without the experience of guilt. Everyone's closet has some skeleton that can justify a certain degree of suffering, and when none can be found, there is always "original sin." But rewards are different, particularly the tangible ones. Blessings "should" only be bestowed upon those who deserve them, and when noncontingent success is extreme, justifying it to oneself is often impossible. Some recipients of "strokes of luck" react as though they have done something illegal; by "beating the odds" or the system, they feel their good fortune is illegitimate.

On the other hand, virtually all people, including recipients of noncontingent success, *would* like to find a justification for accepting any and all positive outcomes that come their way. Remember, virtually everyone, except perhaps those who are already victims of The Success Syndrome and the insane, wants some degree of success. Thus, in the face of noncontingent success, one is strongly motivated to preserve the image of deservedness that comes with striking it rich, if at all possible. Considering the fact that most noncontingent successes do *not* fall into someone's lap totally lacking any justification, this desire is not at all irrational.

Recall that our dart-thrower who scored 50% bull's-eyes knew how to throw the dart and where to aim his throw, and with what level of intensity. Similarly, most boss's sons are taught—from childhood onward—about the firm, its inner workings, management hierarchy, and future goals. In reality, they had at least some form of specialized on-the-job training prior to assuming command. Lucky dart-throwers and boss's sons alike can easily, if so inclined, find some justification for those successes that fall into their laps. They can also find ways of preserving their image of deservedness against tests that pose threats to their favorable self-conceptions.

## DROWNING IN RICHES, THEN BOOZE

Earlier we examined how people initiate self-handi-capping behaviors to preserve their self-image following noncontingent success. In particular, we focused on how people rely on strategically timed alcohol abuse for this purpose. We also noted that self-handicapping strategies typically persist past the point of sustaining an image of deservedness, to destroy the careers and lives of formerly successful individuals. One such supersuccessful individual who was almost destroyed by self-handicapping alcohol abuse is Derek Sanderson.

Derek was no boss's son. From a tough working-class background, he pushed himself through the ranks of Canadian youth hockey leagues—years of contingent and very bruising successes—to earn his way to the Boston Bruins of the National Hockey League. After five grueling years as an NHL player, winning Rookie of the Year honors and contributing significantly to two Stanley Cup championships, Derek was literally atop the world of hockey.

Because of his extraordinary athletic prowess, Derek soon became a media darling, nationally known sports hero, lady's man, and entrepreneur, opening a series of bars and restaurants with the likes of Joe Namath. At the age of 24, he was also "absolutely clean and straight." Derek says he never drank while with the Bruins. But within five years of helping lead Boston to a second world championship, he was to become a skid-row alcoholic who played Russian roulette with a live bullet. He was a classic victim of The Success Syndrome.

Derek's life began to fall apart after he received non-contingent success. Not the kind bestowed on boss's sons or beautiful women, but the *excessive* variety. A material reward so great, so extreme in comparison to that of others, and so far beyond an individual's wildest expectations, that it forced an intensely painful "What did I do to deserve this?" from the "lucky" recipient. To Derek, "Taking the money was the beginning of the end." Prior to that time, he found that being somewhat underpaid for playing hockey and gaining professional recognition devoid of extraneous benefits was a very gratifying life-style:

> I functioned well when I was underpaid, when I was an underdog. It is, you know, the great American way. Plus, *I didn't have any pressure as the underdog.* After I won Rookie of the Year, earning $10,000, they gave me a $1000 raise. No bonus, nothing! For my fifth year with the Bruins, the year we won the second Stanley Cup, I was getting $50,000 and knew I was underpaid. But I also knew that whatever gratification I got, I deserved.

To use Derek's phrase, the beginning of the end came after his fifth year with the Bruins when an upstart group of businessmen decided to form a new hockey league to challenge the NHL. What better way to attract attention to their enterprise and provide legitimacy to the new league than to "steal" the most glamorous, headline-making star of the current Stanley Cup champions, and use him as the centerpiece of the new league? With this end in mind, the owners of the then World Hockey Association Philadelphia Blazers sought to buy Derek Sanderson.

Prior to their pursuing him, Derek had wanted to remain with the Bruins: "I was asking $80,000 for my sixth year, and the Bruins were willing to pay me $75,000, and we were dickering back-and-forth. I was holding out, but I always thought that I'd sign [another contract]." "Philadelphia," as Derek refers to the events that followed, changed everything:

I knew that Philadelphia really wanted me. When I
met with the owners, one began by offering me a $2,300,000
contract. I said, "Well, I've got friends in Boston, night-
clubs, my girlfriend lives there. . . . Moving here will be a
hassle." So [the owner] says, "I am authorized to go as
high as $2,650,000." Now I figure to myself, "This guy gives
me a $350,000 raise in 15 seconds! Shit, why not push the
guy?" So I start deleting this and that from the contract,
taking out whatever parts I don't like. Adding parts like I
have to be captain, etc. I'm going on and on like this and
start thinking, "Shit, I virtually own this team." Then I
said, "OK, give me seven banking days to think about it,"
and I left. I really didn't want to go [to Philadelphia].

Why would a star hockey player who had won awards
documenting his authentic ability to play the game, confident of his own skills and desirous of luxuries and financial security, even *consider* turning down a $2.65 million
contract for one paying $80,000 per year? According to
Derek, even the Bruins' management told him he'd be a
fool to turn his back on an offer that would make him the
highest paid athlete on earth. But Derek didn't want to
hear that from anyone; he wanted friends to persuade him
to remain in Boston:

I knew that [the $2.65 million] contract was too much
money for me. I couldn't earn it; I wasn't worth that kind
of money. Now people find that very difficult to believe,
but *I knew I couldn't earn it and I could start feeling the pressure
building just from getting the offer.* It separated me from the
little fantasy world that I was in and all the protection and
support systems that I had. Taking [the contract] was like
severing ties. I know I sounded like I belonged in a mental
institution, but it was too much, it wasn't right.

The seeds of what would ultimately be the destruction
of Derek's career were planted the year before "Philadel-

phia" in the midst of his second Stanley Cup year with the Bruins. Things were going well for Derek, both on the ice and off: "I had everything I wanted then, a $35,000 salary, fan support and [a girlfriend]. I was in love for the first time." His reaction to feeling this good after years of struggle and pain is a familiar one among those who soon come to suffer from The Success Syndrome:

> I really didn't want to lose [all that I acquired]. I didn't want to die now that things were right. And this fear of flying that I had always had got out of control. I couldn't sleep the night before flights, I got really anxious getting on planes, even thinking about it. So this thing is really getting bad and the Valium and Seconal I'm taking to sleep and relax on the plane are getting me listless, tired all the time, short-tempered with friends. So I went to [a doctor] to tell him about this, and he says, "I don't know anything that is really a better tranquilizer than a shot of good Scotch whiskey." I tell him I never drink and if I do, boom, two beers and I'm out! So he says, "Why don't you try a couple of shots of Scotch before you get on the plane," and I said, "OK."

Derek learned what so many other alcoholics do before their addiction sets in: that alcohol can provide a quick, short-term feeling of relief from anxiety. In Derek's case, it began as a means of helping him overcome his fear of flying. In Boston, he drank only to "self-medicate" prior to an airplane flight. In fact, he so disliked his "medicinal" alcohol that he took it like a pill: washing it down with some sweet soda and then cleansing his mouth with gum. His *self-handicapping* alcohol abuse began once he accepted the Philadelphia contract.

> When I signed with Philadelphia I became lonely and scared. I started to feel inadequate to run [specialized plays]; I hadn't been that offense-minded in Boston, that was Bobby

Orr's job. I missed him as a teammate; who would help me in Philadelphia? Then I'd think about the contract, what they were paying me, and I'd try to think of myself as special, different. I tried to let a superiority complex take over, to believe that I was worth it and could do it alone without my [Bruins] teammates. I felt I had to put myself up on a level that no one else was at, above everybody else, and I had no way to handle the anxiety, no one to turn to for answers. But I had alcohol to relieve me. *It let me keep my high opinion of myself.* On the booze I could show off constantly, I wasn't anxious, didn't fear failing. *Alcohol gave me a false sense of security that I would never fall from the level I was at.*

But fall he did. Derek's esteem-protecting drinking led to alcohol dependence that, in combination with drug abuse and a series of bad business and legal moves, cost him over $15 million. Fortunately, it did not cost him his life. Today, he is a consultant to the Mayor's Advisory Development Commission on Alcohol and Drug Abuse for the Boston City Schools. In addition to his duties promoting responsible attitudes toward alcohol and drugs among vulnerable high school students, Derek is a consultant to a variety of media and business organizations concerned with preventing alcoholism.

Derek made a miraculous recovery from the devastation caused by phenomenal wealth. We see in him a man who was almost destroyed by the doubts and guilt raised by excessive, noncontingent rewards. The sheer enormity of his success, which he tried to resist, threw him into a tailspin of both insecurities and forced self-aggrandizement that nearly ended his life. The pain of *wanting* to believe he was worth the contract he received, and *fearing* he would be exposed as unworthy—to himself and his adoring fans—was too much for him to bear. Self-handicapping alcohol abuse gave him an out, permitting him to sustain his fantasy.

Self-handicappers like Derek Sanderson, who frequently destroy rewarding life-styles and themselves, call to mind a psychiatric disorder known as "moral masochism." Many self-handicappers who must justify excessive favorable outcomes experience intense guilt comparable to that suffered by most moral masochists. In addition, both self-handicappers and moral masochists engage in self-defeating behaviors. Yet despite these similarities and the fact that both disordered states can derive from experiencing success, the disorders are quite distinct.

In contrast to sexual masochism—a perversion that makes sexual satisfaction contingent upon physical or mental pain—moral masochism typically represents an unconscious need for punishment that underlies various types of self-destructive behavior. Whereas the sexual masochist may derive pleasure from beatings, humiliation, or subjugation at the hands of partners, the moral masochist, presumably as a function of excessive unconscious guilt, will resort to self-inflicted "wounds" in situations that would otherwise—for normal individuals—lead to the experience of gratification or increased self-esteem.[4]

Although both men and women manifest sexual and moral masochism, there exists an inaccurate stereotype of the "typical" masochist being a female. This stereotype extends beyond attempts to explain why many women are uncomfortable with success, to blatantly false "interpretations" of women who are victim to various forms of abuse such as wife-battering.

As I have noted throughout this book, particularly in

unfortunate cases like Tennessee Williams and Derek Sanderson, many people—males and females—become paradoxically self-punitive in response to the expectations and pressures derived from attaining success. A regrettable fact of life confronting women in the 1980s is that in addition to the sociocultural factors that have encumbered their success-strivings until recently, they face the additional burden of having to contradict the statements of those women who do make it to the top only to foster the "female/masochist" stereotype by expressing discomfort with what they have achieved.

This problem may be exemplified by Julie Christie reflecting on her status as an Oscar-winning actress. Ms. Christie herself raises the specter of masochism—though denying its presence—revealing her sensitivity to the stereotype. Unfortunately, she does nothing to advance the notion that her suffering is *not* unique to females. Although extreme, her statements are representative of the discomfort experienced by many female successes:

> I couldn't understand winning the Oscar [for *Darling*]. . . . People get cross at me for saying this—I suppose they think it's deliberate masochism, which it isn't. But I've been told that I must practice not to say that I don't deserve the Oscar in order that I won't feel it. . . .
>
> But I *didn't* feel I merited all that success. I was rather ashamed of it, rather embarrassed. The best way I can describe it is—well, I rather saw my success as a sort of scruffy dog, a little mangy dog that's following you around, and you just can't get rid of it! It was a kind of fear that anywhere you went, this little thing was always at your heels. I felt so damned inadequate with almost everybody and everything.[5]

Some women who are undeniable successes like Christie find it difficult to savor their achievements. In our society—which is still in the process of getting comfortable with women who are successful—some women who have made it to the top seem less certain than their male counterparts that they can rest where they are. They seem less willing to define themselves as a "success." Consider the following excerpt from an interview with Connie Chung, the 17-year veteran of TV news who has earned in excess of $350,000 per year as an anchor for NBC *News at Sunrise* and the NBC *Nightly News* on Saturdays:

> REPORTER: To what do you attribute your success?
>
> CHUNG: I don't think I'm successful. . . .
>
> REPORTER: Come on. . . .
>
> CHUNG: It's presumptuous to declare success, and I find people who do so obnoxious. Men are more apt to label themselves successful than women are. A man will say "I'm a success." . . . But no matter what kind of woman you talk to, no matter what her profession, she is more humble about things. . . .[6]

The "humility" that Chung and countless successful women like her manifest to the public is often construed as a surface manifestation of moral (*not* sexual) masochism. "Why wouldn't someone as successful as she declare success unless she were determined to undermine it or turn her accomplishments into agony," the lay reasoning goes. This was a perspective expressed by many of those who wrote to me in 1984 after *The Boston Globe* published stories about my Executive Stress Clinic and "Karen" (not her real name), a female patient of mine.[7]

As it turns out, those who wrote to me were correct—Karen was a masochist, both morally and sexually. My concern over the letters stemmed from the fact that many writers attributed her disorder to her gender, not the true causal factor, her upbringing. Were Karen a Kenneth instead, *he* would have most probably developed a very similar character structure given the upbringing Karen was exposed to. The story about Karen—written by a skilled reporter who was not an expert in mental health—presented a graphic description of how she suffered from excessive success. What it failed to do was describe why, and in so doing, inadvertently fostered the stereotype of female successes being masochistic.

When Karen entered therapy, she was a 30-year-old vice president for a nationally known corporation with a Boston division, which she headed. Her base salary was $165,000 per year, but with bonuses she earned in excess of $200,000. She was an individual whom the *Globe* reporter described as ". . . an intelligent, attractive woman who exudes a brisk, successful aura"[8]—an understatement. Karen is an exceptionally talented and successful woman who, in the past, reacted to every success she experienced by entering into a relationship—either professionally or sexually—with people who would abuse or inflict pain upon her. Thankfully, that pattern appears to have ended as a result of her hard work in psychotherapy.

Now, as then, Karen agreed to have her story told provided she is guaranteed anonymity. She feels particularly vulnerable—as a *female* executive—to the damage that could result from being identified as someone who once suffered a psychological disturbance. What follows is some of what she told the reporter, and some details about her history, which account for her experience of The Success Syndrome:

> Women of our generation were not raised to be successful. When we are, we think we have to pay our dues. I was raised to work hard for what I got. I didn't think there would be a payoff like this. The higher it is, the more pain is involved because I don't think I deserve it. . . .

I feel I have to apologize for it. I head a large division of a large company . . . I guess I'm supposed to say I'm very good at what I do. My concept is that someone who makes that kind of money has to be perfect. My father made $13,000 a year, supported nine children and worked a second job at night. I really admire him. I put myself through school, worked hard—I worked 40 hours a week getting my MBA nights, too—but it turned out to be easy in business. I look at things quickly and practically. . . . I do something satisfactorily, and they give me more money, more responsibility and more promotions. Sometimes I think it's more than I deserve. I once turned down a raise. After I did it, I couldn't sleep at night. . . .

Women's libbers say, "Experience your success." I'm sorry, I can't say that I experience it. At times I say, "Wow! I did a lot, they're pressing money on me, giving me a title." Then I say, "Wait a minute, I didn't do that." Women get high enough and then fail. I found that out by talking to other successful women. It's a common topic they don't admit to men.[9]

Karen's discomfort with success was intense, and as noted above, she responded to it by entering into punitive relationships (at work or with men) when she had achieved a significant goal. But she wasn't simply a successful woman who periodically succumbed to the burden of expectations derived from representing her "sisters" atop a status hierarchy—despite the fact that those expectations are excessive and typically stress-inducing. Karen's disorder stemmed from a childhood marked by a status that is almost always a mixed blessing: She was her father's favorite.

We are familiar with the biblical Joseph, who, marked as his father's favorite, suffered the consequence of exile. Karen became a "marked" member of her family and suffered her own negative consequences. As a youth, she was the only one of nine children who shared her father's interest in model building. Because of this, Karen received the lion's share of his free time and attention. On the positive side, it is likely that this involvement with her father, and "favorite daughter" status, played a significant role in Karen's developing the motivation that propelled her throughout life. At some significant level, she has the self-confidence that Freud attributed to being a "favorite" child.

On the other, wholly negative side, Karen's siblings were more than merely rivalrous when she and her father retired to the family room workshop; they committed overtly hostile acts. Karen became the target of verbal and physical abuse linked directly to her being "daddy's helper." On one occasion, when her parents went out of town, two of her sisters held her prisoner in her bedroom and taunted her for two days. Given the set of incompatible consequences that Karen experienced from model building—paternal adoration and intense sibling hostility—it is no wonder that her adult accomplishments generated intensely ambivalent feelings.

In her statements to *The Boston Globe,* and throughout the initial stages of her psychotherapy, Karen indicated that she felt she didn't "deserve" success. At a deeper level of feeling, she didn't *want* it and, in fact, feared its consequences. Having learned as a child that being selected "from the pack" as a "favorite"—a situtation that parallels the adult experience of being promoted—would lead to both good and bad outcomes, Karen retained ambivalent feelings about success. Her symptom—entering into masochistic relationships following success—can be understood as replicating the pattern of abuse that she suffered at the hands of her brothers and sisters. As an adult, Karen had relationships with men who would degrade her in public or in bed, a pattern that paralleled the degradation she suffered when growing up. Although this is a significant psychological disorder—one of the more commonly observed negative consequences of "favorite child" status—*it is in no way a gender-based disorder.*

A male patient of mine, Charles, is a 35-year-old corporate VP who cannot tolerate being successful. He entered psychotherapy to address the fact that whenever he is about to achieve success in either his love life or his work life—the two most important spheres of existence for normal psychological functioning according to Freud—he sabotages relationships in the other sphere. At those times when his career was ascending, he would wreck good relationships by acting in a variety of inappropriate ways guaranteed to alienate his psychologically healthy lovers. On the two occasions when he was on the verge of getting married, Charles created so much interpersonal turmoil at his workplace that it nearly cost him his very promising career.

Although Charles's disordered life-style is not identical to Karen's, similarities do abound. The most striking parallel is the guilt and subsequent self-sabotage they both manifest following success. Charles is as self-punitive and masochistic as Karen, and in no way suffers this disorder as a result of gender confusion. He is a male with masochistic tendencies, and is also a victim of The Success Syndrome.

The profound difficulties with success suffered by Karen and Charles, like those of Derek Sanderson, point to the multitude of problems that result from success. Yet we should remember that both Derek and my patients suffered extreme versions of reactions that anyone could experience on a more moderate level after achieving success.

Anyone who succeeds suffers some degree of social isolation and jealousy as Karen did as a child. The guilt motivating Charles's self-sabotage is a consequence of unresolved Oedipal conflicts, which—in both greater and lesser degress—hamper the lives of untold thousands of people. Similarly, all who achieve highly significant successes suffer from the burden of living up to their own reputations and astronomical salaries, as in the case of Derek. Victims of The Success Syndrome do not suffer from unique pressures or expectations; they do suffer the burden of expectations more intensely.

There are many reasons why people react as differently to success as Bob Lobel and Derek Sanderson did. Much of the responsibility or "blame" can be attributed to the nature of the success one receives. Noncontingent successes are always more difficult to handle than contingent ones. Yet both Derek and Bob had *earned* their huge rewards. There must be factors other than the rewards that account for why their reactions to success were as disparate as those reported earlier for playwrights Moss Hart and Tennessee Williams.

If we look closely at the "fine print" of the contracts that Derek had with "Philadelphia" and Bob with WBZ-TV, we will see that Derek's "package" was for slightly more money—and contained far more pressure. To begin with, the upstart World Hockey Association Philadelphia Blazers were buying Derek to legitimize and advertise the *entire* league. They wanted to compete with the NHL, and needed Derek to do this. While this was not an explicit agreement between Derek and the WHA, it was certainly obvious to all concerned parties. Bob Lobel's contract, in stark contrast to Derek's, contained a mandate that he sustain *his* award-winning performance, not assume the responsibility for giving life to a fledgling TV station. The corporation was flourishing when Bob received his contract. His success or failure was his alone; if he went down, he would not take many dependents with him.

In my definition of The Success Syndrome, I indicated that success imposes a variety of burdensome expectations on those who reach the top. One of the more burdensome of these is the obligation to support or assist others. When we compare the respective successes of Derek Sanderson and Bob Lobel, we can see that although their tangible rewards were comparable, the burden of expectations imposed upon Derek was far greater. Since stress is produced by performance demands—not the inherent nature of a stimulus—we can understand that Derek, exposed to greater expectations, would be exposed to more stress. Thus, one explanation for why success derailed Derek and not Bob is, quite simply, that Derek's success was inherently more stressful.

There is another aspect of their contracts that can explain Derek's demise and Bob's prosperity: in a word, diversification. We noted earlier, in our discussion of depressions following success, that many successes wonder "where do I go from here?" once they have attained a significant goal. The pain of this circumstance is felt most intensely by those who have attained success in careers that exploit only one talent. Athletes are the prototypic victims of these sorts of depressions. But overspecialized scientists, engineers, salespeople, and others whose careers involve only one product or "market" suffer comparable fates if, for whatever reason, their grants, markets, or abilities cease to exist. In fact, any professional who devotes himself exclusively to his career—a workaholic executive being a prime example—is likely to be devastated if he suffers a detour on, or closing of, his career path. Derek Sanderson, a hockey player for most of his life, knew that his present and future prosperity depended solely on his doing one thing with phenomenal skill. Were he unable, for any reason, to execute that skill, he would forfeit his pot of gold.

Although Bob Lobel contracted to be a sportscaster, not a jack-of-all-trades, his duties within the role of sportscaster are more diversified. In addition to reporting on the 6 and 11 o'clock newscasts, he broadcasts a variety of live sporting events (as a play-by-play announcer) and develops special reports that extend beyond "mere" sportscasting. While it's true that Bob would have to seek different work were he to permanently lose his voice, his fate is definitely not as dependent upon one type of performance as Derek's. Should the ratings of Bob's sportscasts ever fall, he could recoup some of that loss with "blockbuster" special reports, dazzling play-by-play, or other reportorial projects. And if all else failed, Bob could rely on his M.Ed., permitting him to attempt a career in teaching. Given the nature of Derek Sanderson's occupation, skills, and background, diversification—though possible—is far more difficult to envision and execute.

Being limited in the options one has for sustaining a sense of positive self-esteem is stressful. When you have all of your "eggs in one basket," the well-being of that basket is more critical than would be the case were several baskets at your disposal. Stated in terms of performance demands, your feeling of competence is far less vulnerable if you have three chances to hit a bull's-eye as opposed to just one.

There are doubtless a variety of other explanations as to why certain people can resist the effects of The Success Syndrome and why others cannot. Some individuals are simply more stress-resistant owing to their basic personality.[10] However, the truly stress-resistant are rare; most of us do succumb to stress on occasion, and when that stress is derived from success, special psychotherapeutic strategies are often needed. A program designed to address the disorders deriving from success will be presented in the next chapter.

Part Four

# TREATING THE SUCCESS SYNDROME IN INDIVIDUALS AND CORPORATIONS

Chapter Twelve

# THE EXECUTIVE STRESS CLINIC

*Men are disturbed not by things, but by the views they take of them.*

Epictetus

*We do not succeed in changing things according to our desire, but gradually our desire changes. The situation that we hoped to change because it was intolerable becomes unimportant.*

Marcel Proust

Had he been so inclined, Epictetus, a philosopher who plied his trade sometime between 50 and 120 A.D., could have served as a theoretical consultant to the first stress clinic. He certainly understood the most crucial aspect of stress, namely, perceptions. His insight into what constitutes a stressful or "disturbing" situation or "thing" is 100% accurate. Nothing *in and of itself* causes stress; our *interpretations* of events, interactions, and other aspects of our environment are what cause stress reactions.

Proust, on the other hand, with his interest in "change," is more the lay clinician. His maxim is an attempt to apply the insight of Epictetus to a person experiencing stress or psychological conflict. In essence, Proust has offered an explanation for the effectiveness of the "grandmotherly" prescription of waiting for time to heal all wounds. The pain of wounds—typically from broken hearts or crushed egos—diminishes over time because as we mature, we are able to reevaluate "intolerable" events and see them for what they now are, and probably always were: disappointments that could be adapted to with relative ease.

Although the insights of Epictetus and Proust encapsulate the fundamental tenets of any stress management program, they have particular relevance as therapeutic

strategies for those who suffer from The Success Syndrome. Since virtually all of the disorders that result from
success can be traced to distorted *perceptions* of what is, or
will be, expected as a consequence of succeeding, the focus
of treatment to address these problems must be on altering
"the views men take of things." Specifically, the most effective approach to eliminate "the stress of success" is to
correct the way in which a successful individual comes to
perceive himself and those around him immediately after
he climbs from the ranks of the striving to those of the
successful.

## THE QUESTION OF COMPETENCY
## VERSUS EXPECTANCY

Despite repeated attempts to define psychological stress
for what it is—a performance demand that exceeds an
individual's *perceived* competency to meet that demand—
lay and professional people alike continually assume that
stressed people suffer from some *behavorial* deficiency or
lack of competency. For individuals with minimal levels
of intelligence, training, or skill, this may in fact be true.
Life is more stressful if one cannot manifest a skill capable
of netting a job and a livelihood. Similarly, if an individual
lacks so-called "social skills"—the capactiy to interact with
others in an empathic and mutually satisfying manner—
life becomes more stressful. He finds it difficult or impossible to secure the cooperation of others to complete tasks
that cannot be completed alone. The maxim "no man is
an island" has relevance here. People find life far less demanding and stressful when others willingly offer to facilitate their tasks—from carrying packages to planning a
trip to an unknown locale—than when totally isolated and
left to their own devices.

Expectancies and *distorted* perceptions are central and crucial to the disorders deriving from success for one simple reason: few people rise to the top of an organizational hierarchy without many apparent skills that make tasks relatively simple to perform. Even boss's sons, daughters, and spouses will reliably manifest a distinct skill, if only a pleasing style that comes from "proper breeding." Thus, the particular aspect of a successful person's life that leads to the experience of stress is not a demand to perform competently; he can, and has done so in the past. The stress in a successful person's life derives from the *perception* or *belief* that he *should* perform at an ever-increasing level of competence. As we have seen repeatedly, once a person achieves a significant goal, he comes to believe, as do friends and associates, that he possesses an overall level of competence that cuts across *all* situations and that he can call upon whenever it is required.

This inevitable expectation to replicate or exceed past performances is burden enough. An additional fear for many is that as they continue to climb the ladder of success, they will become more socially isolated. To a significant degree this is true. Many who feel "lonely at the top" isolate themselves, suspecting that subordinates who befriend them have ulterior motives. Other successful people believe that the only reason others care for them is because of their capacity to bring about successes. Regardless of why certain successful people become isolated, social isolation and the subsequent loss of "helping hands" breed greater stress.

## ATTRIBUTIONS

Epictetus said it first, and it has been confirmed innumerable times since: psychological stress exists because

people *believe* something about themselves and their world.
Despite the fact that a person's beliefs, opinions, attitudes,
and the expectancies they generate, may be totally false
or inaccurate, these beliefs still govern the outcome of all
social interactions. Stressful stimuli, much like beauty, exist totally "in the eye of the beholder." Hence, therapeutic
strategies for eliminating stress must, first and foremost,
deal with the "eye of the beholder." More specifically,
therapists addressing stress-related disorders must first
understand how debilitating expectations develop, and then
design strategies to eliminate them or substitute a healthier
set of expectations.

   In all instances where a person forms an attitude or
a belief abut himself, his world, or other individuals, "attributional processes" are taking place.[1] Simply stated,
attributional processes answer the naturally occurring
question, "why did an action occur, and why did it take
a particular form?"[2] At a deeper level of analysis, attributional processes attempt to discern whether an event
occurred because of "external" environmental factors (e.g.,
social pressures or intense physical stimuli), or the "internal" qualities of an individual (e.g., abilities, attitudes). An
individual tries to discern what caused a behavior or event
so he can predict, for the future, how interacting with
particular people and particular environments will affect
him.[3]

   Psychologists who have studied attributional processes have developed a series of rules that specify how
people systematically determine the underlying causes of
behaviors. Several of these rules have a direct relevance
to the treatment strategies I have developed for individuals
suffering from The Success Syndrome. Underlying all of
these treatments is the attributional law pertaining to "extremes" of behavior. Specifically, behaviors that are out-

of-the-ordinary, exceptional, or unexpected generate stronger attributions (to an individual) than behaviors that are commonplace or ordinary. Stated another way, the only time we can assume that a behavior is reflective of a person's dispositions—abilities, attitudes, and psychological makeup—is when it deviates from social norms.[4]

Observers learn nothing about what a person is really like if he or she follows social convention and remains one of the crowd. However, we can learn a lot about "the cut of someone's jib" if his behaviors are not in accordance with social constraints. We draw a "dispositional attribution" from a person's public nudity ("he's an exhibitionist") if he is naked at a White House dinner party (where "black-tie" is the standard attire), but can make no such inference with any confidence if the same behavior is observed at a nudist colony. Similarly, we can attribute great intellectual prowess to an individual who has solved a puzzle if that puzzle is Rubik's cube (which only a few people can solve) as opposed to tic-tac-toe.

The successful, whose behavior is definitely "extreme," frequently find themselves in a position where they must contend with a set of attributions they were unaware of having generated. Without setting out to garner labels such as "star," "hero," or "role model," successful people find that their talents have created "attributional monsters" that develop with an energy of their own.

In an earlier discussion of implicit personality theories and the "halo effect" that results from success, I indicated how star athletes who are expected to be after-dinner speakers are unwitting victims of the attributions that their exceptional talents generate. Similarly, supersuccessful businessmen are regularly expected to join boards of directors for charities and advise civic-minded organizations despite the fact that their talents (e.g., investing, marketing) may be unrelated to anything outside of their business activities. As a result of the "extreme" behaviors they manifest, these successful people are constantly saddled with attributions that they neither sought nor prepared for, but nevertheless must cope with.

Another attributional principle relevant to the concerns of an Executive Stress Clinic is called the "discounting principle."[5] Simply stated, it maintains that when a behavior can be attributed to several plausible causes, we are less able to derive an attribution than would be the case were only one "plausible cause" available. For example, we would find it nearly impossible to judge a person's level of "extroversion" or interest in socializing from his presence at an office Christmas party since attending such functions is usually mandatory or, at a minimum, expected. In this instance, any given attendee may be an extrovert who likes to "party," or a conformist who merely wishes to "fit in" with the corporate image and not offend his boss. However, if the same partygoer were observed at *every* party advertised on the office bulletin board, the only possible explanation for such invariant behavior would be an "internal" or personal trait such as extroversion.

*One Caveat.* Expectancies and attributional processes are the core components of The Success Syndrome that I address at my Executive Stress Clinic. Before I proceed further on the question of how these processes apply to issues of therapeutic interventions, however, I must note that in cases of psychiatric disorders such as self-handicapping alcohol abuse, success depression, and severe social isolation, intensive psychotherapy, beyond the procedures described below, is required. The basic clinical interventions designed to treat the problems created by

The Success Syndrome should be viewed as the therapeutic equivalent to planting seeds. Before the land will bear fruit, irrigation, cultivation, and adequate sunlight are necessary. More delicate crops—like more severe problems—would require individualized attention to achieve an appropriate resolution.

## BASIC APPROACHES TO COMBATING THE STRESS OF SUCCESS

*I. How to Control the Demands Derived from Success: Avoiding the "What Do I Do for an Encore?" Phenomenon.* An innate tendency of all humans who strive for success is to raise their personal performance standards each time they attain a previously set goal.[6] This is also one of the fundamental reasons why successful people experience stress. Once they have reached their particular goal, any "encore" that is not at a "higher" level will either be a subjective failure or, at best, merely status quo. As an individual's level of success rises, so do the possibilities for encountering failure or emptiness in subsequent strivings for greater success.

The individual who has made the transition from the status of "striving for success" to "having succeeded" is particularly vulnerable to the various forms of stress that result from the nagging concern, "what do I do for an encore?" Leaving aside the fact that repeating successful performances is extremely difficult, we can list countless careers in which merely "doing it again, only better" just will not work. Creative people, particularly writers and artists, must develop new projects after the success of a book or painting; "sequels" are possible (e.g., Sylvester Stallone's *Rocky* movies) but precarious routes to sustained success.

Scientists suffer a similar fate since merely refining aspects of one's own previously successful research ("extending the paradigm" as it is known in the trade), does not ensure one's prominence within the scientific community. Recall the Goodrich tire commercial depicting the designer of the 721 radial and the cleaning woman who confronts him at his drafting table to ask what he plans to do next. The look of devastation on the engineer's face, wrought by that question, is a common occurrence among scores of talented people who, at the pinnacle of their success, must achieve something new.

Since no therapeutic program currently in existence can reliably train people to be creative, insightful, or inspired, the most effective coping strategy for victims of The Success Syndrome stressed by the need to perform an encore is a "proactive" approach. Stated another way, the best means of avoiding the stress derived of expected encore performances is never to confine yourself to one stage, arena, or proving ground. There is no need to improve upon a particular achievement if you have multiple avenues for success at your disposal. In short, a successful person can avoid the stress precipitated by demands for an encore if his creative energies and achievement strivings are *diversified*.

Humble psychologists will tell you—with tongue partially embedded in cheek—that most of the principles guiding psychological research and psychotherapy have actually been "discovered" by grandmothers. The therapeutic strategy designed for victims of "encore expectations" is, to a large extent, a variant of the "don't put all your eggs in one basket" philosophy. Translated for the career needs of entrepreneurs, scientists, artists, and others who intend to climb the ladder of success, the proactive strategy of choice to avoid encore expectations is to have multiple projects going on simultaneously. In this way, once you successfully complete one project, another work "in progress" will already be in the wings.

In the preceding chapter I argued that one reason why Bob Lobel was *not* a victim of The Success Syndrome was because he had *the potential* for diversification available to him. The mere fact of being in a position where one is able to sustain a successful status through more than one activity can relieve the pressure of encore expectations. There is, however, an obvious risk run by those who actually *enact* a proactive approach to avoiding encore expectations; namely, workaholism born of *over*diversification. A good friend of mine, who is a prominent psychologist with a national reputation, suffers from this disorder. He literally has more "irons in the fire" than one man can possibly handle, and he invariably finds himself stressed by his inability to keep up with the day-to-day performance demands of his correspondence, committee meetings, and wife. In his case, despite his never suffering from encore expectations, he is so overextended that he rarely has time to enjoy the successes he achieves.

A similar concern raised by victims of The Success Syndrome who are urged to diversify is the fear of diluting their energies and "spreading themselves too thin." While this risk is real for workaholics, it is rare that moderate levels of diversification will deprive an individual of the capacity to achieve successful outcomes. One need only look as far as the venture capital community—where capitalists of every stripe juggle several potential projects simultaneously—to realize that shifting one's attention from project to project does not necessarily diminish the *quality* of the attention given to a task, only the quantity.

The process of diversification can best be accomplished by broadening one's range of options *within* a given area of expertise. In the case of Bob Lobel described earlier, he was able to participate in a number of different broadcasting activities, thereby enhancing his opportunities for success. In a similar manner, my friends in the venture capital community are always involved in a number of projects, but these typically relate to one *central* theme such as genetic engineering, computer technology, health service organizations, or communications. A specialist in the field of health service organizations would certainly be expected to seek funding for several different hospital projects at any given time, but would not, if sensible, diversify too far afield—into an unrelated specialization such as communications, for example. Were an executive looking to diversify his activities as a means of "inoculating" himself against encore expectations, he would be wise to expand his activities within one range of activities (e.g., marketing, finance, operations) that he knew best.

My clinical experience has, however, demonstrated that there is a great deal of potential benefit to adding a hobby or avocational pursuit to your schedule if you anticipate significant pressures to sustain success. Self-esteem is all too frequently derived from only one activity, thereby rendering an individual vulnerable to major psychological difficulties should that activity no longer be available as a source of building self-esteem. Derek Sanderson discovered this as his career began to slip. Many other successful people feel this on an ongoing basis as their business organizations shift the corporate focus away from their particular area of expertise.

Diversification strategies that center around adding hobbies or recreational pursuits to one's life will probably never compensate fully for the loss of esteem or gratification suffered from encore expectations or flagging success rates. It is true, nevertheless, that they can *bolster* a stressed or sagging sense of self-esteem. It is very important, as we shall see below, that successful people realize that they are more than what they are "branded" by their careers. Avocations such as organized athletic pursuits, community organizations, or hobbies enable a successful person to derive satisfaction from activities outside his career, which reduce—intermittently—the pressure placed upon sustaining success within one's area of expertise.

The one drawback to using avocations as alternative sources of self-esteem comes from those instances in which the individual tries to turn an amateur's enjoyment into a substitute career. A CEO may derive an enormous amount of pleasure from discussing the importance of his corporation on TV programs such as *Nightline* or *60 Minutes*. He may even prove to be an entertaining guest. But not every CEO is a born anchorperson. Were a CEO to assume that because of his sporadic appearances on television he could become the next Ted Koppel, he would find his attempts to achieve his dream typically less than gratifying.

The proactive approach that I advocate for preempting "where do I go from here?" phenomena follows the principle of "all things in moderation." Patients at the Executive Stress Clinic I direct participate in a series of didactic and interactive group meetings that involve evaluations of their performance capabilities as well as opportunities for initiating simultaneous projects. In addition, these therapy groups focus on a form of cognitive behavior therapy[7] called "reattribution training"—a therapeutic technique that attempts to change a person's inappropriate and self-defeating thoughts. Simply stated, reattribution training challenges the validity of unrealistic performance standards a person sets for himself. More important, if successful, reattribution training techniques can enable a stressed patient to develop a new set of healthy performance standards that permit him to strive for realistic, nonthreatening goals.[8] Below is a sampling of the topics addressed in reattribution training:

A. *Directed Challenges to the Expectations Derived from Success.* The concept of implicit personality theories is examined and refuted in an attempt to have patients recognize that success in one realm of life need not be predictive of success in all realms. This axiom is the initial component of reattribution training because it sets the stage for subsequent attempts to have patients adopt diversified approaches to their careers. Were the topic of generalized expectancies not refuted, a patient might fear that he would have to excel in all aspects of his diversified career because he had previously been successful in one endeavor. Acceptance of *invalid* expectancies derived from implicit personality theories is the dominant cause of a patient's refusal to attempt diversifying his achievement goals.

B. *Redirecting Attention to the Process of Succeeding as Opposed to the Products of Success.* Earlier, as part of the discussion dealing with losses inherent in success, we examined how many successful people reviewed their careers and found that the climb to the top was more gratifying than "arriving." Bob Lobel made a similar observation when he complained about the manner in which achieving "star" status in his field transformed him from a "producer" into a "consumer." Despite the fact that the fruits of success are sweet, they do not totally erase memories of the joy inherent in acquiring "the fruit."

Those victims of The Success Syndrome suffering from encore expectations no longer have the joy of looking forward to a climb to the top. For one thing, they have already succeeded. Moreover, they become overly concerned with greater levels of accomplishment as a result of their success. This diverts their attention from enjoying the project that brought them their initial success. By readjusting their attributions toward the potential pleasures inherent in working toward a goal versus attaining one, the initially rocky road to career diversification is paved. Thoughts of working on a variety of projects inevitably assume greater rewarding potential than that offered by attempts to comply with encore expectations in one restricted endeavor.

These, and several other reattribution training techniques, enable patients to examine, and, in many cases, adopt, a positive attitude toward diversifying their careers. There is no magic inherent in these techniques, only a few simple (yet nevertheless effective) principles of psychology at work. The fundamental psychological "law" that underlies the strategy of diversification argues that success is a process involving both the pursuit of a goal and achievements that represent ends to that *pursuit.*

Victims of success who are stressed by encore expectations lose sight of the fact that *both* aspects of the *process* can be rewarding. By diversifying and maintaining multiple ongoing endeavors, a successful person (1) need not adhere to expectatons that he perform an encore at a higher level of proficiency (since his energies are committed to several ongoing tasks), and (2) need not suffer the loss of reward inherent in success since he is constantly being gratified by his involvement in the *process* of developing several *potentially* successful projects. The true beauty of diversification strategies is that success in every ongoing activity is *never* expected. A certain percentage of failure is tolerable—even anticipated—when there is more than one iron in the fire.

*II. How to Accept Affection and Admiration following Success: Solving the "Is It Who I Am or What I Did?" Riddle.* The investment firm of Merrill Lynch touts its competency through advertising campaigns that feature a bull and the motto "A Breed Apart." As noted earlier, being distinct from the herd is often a mark of success since dominance, independence, and even distinctiveness are earmarks of the individual who has risen to the top. But being distinct from the herd or alone at the top can also leave an individual deprived of a great many rewarding experiences that would otherwise have been his had he been able to "run with the pack." Thus, many successful people are deprived of the luxury of camaraderie and consequently suffer from loneliness.

At the outset of this chapter I noted that there are two scenarios that account for successful people experiencing social isolation: (1) they assume that the friendly gestures of subordinates are initiated for ulterior motives such as securing influence, favors, or the like, or (2) they maintain the belief that without their success they would be "nothing"; hence, they must constantly work to sustain success and its by-product—the affection of others. Although these two causes of social isolation appear to be totally independent and distinct, they actually derive from success consuming the thoughts of individuals experiencing the pressures of The Success Syndrome. These people come to regard success as the only positive aspect of their life.

Because they believe that others like them for what they have done (e.g., become CEO of a corporation; written a prize-winning play), as opposed to who they are (e.g., a caring person with wit and charm), many successful people shut themselves off from social contacts to avoid being exploited. Frequently, concerns of this sort are justifiable. Sycophants inhabit every corner of the globe and are eager to prey upon the naive individual who has attained success. Gold diggers do marry for money, and in corporations "yes-men" are the rule, not the exception. (A friend explained the origin of the term "yuppie" by noting that this group of status-seekers responds to any directive, reprimand, or abuse from superiors with, "Yup, yup, yup, yup . . . anything you say.") But the prejudice that any individual who is beneath them in a status hierarchy will necessarily "kiss-up" with manipulative intent robs a successful person of deriving satisfaction from social relationships with those of lower status even when their feelings are genuine.

The sad story of Tennessee Williams illustrates just how destructive and painful the mistrust born of success can be. In Williams's extreme case—which was probably exacerbated by a host of underlying psychological disorders—being unable to relate to friends and associates led to a ruinous deterioration of his life. Although most victims of The Success Syndrome do not experience devastation comparable to that suffered by Williams, distress derived from the "do they love me for who I am *or* what I did?" dilemma is one of the more common adverse consequences of success, and one that is not easily resolved.

The treatment program that I have developed for victims of success who cannot derive satisfaction from interpersonal relationships has two foci: (1) the passivity born of being "at the top," and (2) the tendency of successful people to define themselves in terms of their success. By instituting reattribution therapy for these two distorted perspectives, I have found that successful people can overcome the social distance that they invariably impose between themselves and subordinates—even those who sincerely care.

A. *Reversing the "Natural" Tendency toward Being Passive in Interpersonal Relationships following Success.* Successful people are courted, befriended, and pursued for their power and influence by those who are less successful. Although these may not be the only reasons, they are often the overriding ones. This is a well-known fact of life. What is less well known are the negative consequences of being in a position where you are constantly "sought out" and are virtually never required to do the "seeking."

Since successful people rarely experience a *need* to initiate social contacts, their perspective on most of their social interactions is significantly different from that of those who routinely seek them out. A common occurrence among victims of The Success Syndrome who are socially isolated is that they come to devalue and view with disdain those individuals who constantly seek their attention, company, or social contact. The scorn that successful people develop for those who pursue them is a naturally occurring psychological response to being in a position where they never have a need to initiate social contacts.

Psychological research has provided conclusive proof that people come to like and appreciate what they have worked hard or suffered for.[9] Fraternities exploit this principle in their hazing and initiation rituals: Pledges are expected to manifest loyalty to, and liking for, the brotherhood in direct proportion to the amount of energy, effort, and suffering required to earn admission to the group. A related application of this principle can be found in all dating advice books or in the advice passed along from mothers to daughters: play "hard-to-get!" The theory underlying this maxim is that boys (men) are more attracted to women who place obstacles in the way of dates and withhold affection than to "easy" women who fall all over themselves when asked for a date.

The problem with playing hard-to-get—in either social

interactions or business settings—is that it can, and often does, backfire. Not that suitors get discouraged in their pursuit of "Ms. Right"; if she's "right" they'll be persistent. The problem is that Ms. Right will often question the worthiness of many potential "Mr. Rights" based on the ease with which their affection is obtained. If the rule of thumb is, "you work hard for *good* things," a logical corollary is that things that are cast into your lap or come to you through no effort—like junk mail—must not be too valuable.

This principle applies to people as well as possessions. Groucho Marx purportedly claimed that he would refuse membership in any club that would accept him. Why pay dues to join a group that would admit "anybody" like him? Circumstances that force successful people into making this type of attributional error cost them the friendship of countless worthwhile people who, for whatever reason, are eager to establish friendships or, by a quirk of fate, are their subordinates.

Many successful people are cast into roles that are functionally equivalent to that of "Ms. Right" for a variety of suitors. As a consequence, without realizing how or why it is occurring, a successful person can develop contempt for those who court him. Finding himself persistently pursued without reciprocal efforts on his own behalf forces the successful person to address the most fundamental of all attributional questions: why a particular act (everyone calling him for social reasons) has occurred. Stated another way, discovering that he is being sought out as though he were Mr. Right by a variety of suitors, a successful person must determine if the attention is because the suitors are deprived of dates or because he is special.

Pyschologists tell us that attributional analyses cease when an individual discovers what is called "reason enough." That is, we stop analyzing why an event occurred when a satisfactory attribution has been drawn, whether it is accurate or not.[10] In the case of successful people attempting to account for the behavior of subordinates who court them, the most salient and accessible attribution that can be made is: "They want me for my success (money, power, influence). . . . If *they* were worthwhile social contacts, I'd be calling them!" Despite protestations from others that may contradict this inference, a successful person has a hard time looking beyond this highly plausible attributional analysis.

Correcting the rational—albeit flawed—attribution that social contacts from subordinates are initiated only for ulterior motives is difficult when an individual sits atop a hierarchy and all social initiatives are directed at him. One of the simplest, and most effective, approaches to this problem is arranging for victims of The Success Syndrome—who are blocked from experiencing favorable social interactions—to initiate social contacts with subordinates in contexts other than those in which their status discrepancies are salient. To the extent that this is possible, the successful person can be dealt with in an arena that forces him from the "what I did" to the "who I am" status, thereby permitting an unencumbered exchange of feelings.

This type of interaction is clearly not simple to arrange outside of controlled environments, and it is typically not possible to initiate with subordinates prior to some form of professional intervention. But it is possible to begin this process with groups of successful people who are participating in structured clinical programs. The advantage of teaching these individuals to initiate social contacts in group therapy sessions derives from the fact that all participants have some executive status, and have some success, so they cannot exploit their power or influence over other members of the group.

Having a group of successful people interacting on neutral turf dissolves familiar status hierarchies. Successful businesspeople, physicians, attorneys, academics, and athletes are all on an equal footing in a clinical setting, a situation that is rarely replicated in the outside world where Wall Street, universities, courtrooms, and various athletic fields each have their own unique pecking order. This creates an incredibly awkward feeling for those accustomed to dominating group meetings, but is extremely helpful when the aim of an interaction is to enable participants to exchange authentic feelings.

The specific aim of stripping an Executive Stress Clinic patient of his *external* trappings of success and requiring him to be the *initiator* of social interactions is to eliminate the influence of any factor other than "internal" personal variables that could affect the reactions of others. In the various role-playing exercises that I have designed for this particular phase of the Executive Stress Clinic's programming (e.g., *asking for*, not demanding help; soliciting corrective feedback), patients reexperience the consequences of seeking the support of others. With no reason other than "who I am" to account for why they are being treated in a particular manner—good or bad—attributions centering around the exploitative motives of others no longer meet the criterion of "reason enough." Victims of The Success Syndrome who enter this track of group psychotherapy are forced—some for the first time in memory—to receive and accept interpersonal feedback for what it is intended to be: a reflection of what others think of them as people, not as occupants of seats of power.

B. *Learning That You Are More Than an Extremely Successful Butcher, Baker, or Candlestick Maker.* Common knowledge maintains that "actions speak louder than words" and "by your deeds shall ye be known." Not surprisingly, psychologists have proven these insights to be true. In a series of experiments designed to determine how people form attributions of others, psychologists found that a person's behavior exerted more influence over others' judgments of him than any other type of information.[11] The flip side of this phenomenon is true as well. In psychological studies of what is called "*self*-attribution"— how people use the rules of attribution theory to form their self-conceptions—a person's actual behavior is the most potent determinant of what he thinks and feels about himself.[12] Descartes's maxim, "*Cogito, ergo sum*" (I think, therefore I am) is severely qualified by psychological research. Sartre's viewpoint that man is the sum of his acts seems to prevail. Far more frequently than not, people behave in a particular manner and *then* conclude who they are from reviewing what they have done, as opposed to determining who they are and then acting accordingly.[13]

This psychological "truth" has obvious implications for those who suffer from The Success Syndrome. Anyone who has earned an authentic success has very likely devoted enormous amounts of time and energy in pursuit of that goal. To paraphrase T. E. Lawrence, "there could be no satisfaction in an easily acquired success." According to the laws of self-attribution theory, the attitudes that a person holds about himself as a professional, particularly if that profession has brought him success, should be positive. Like the rest of us, the successful person comes to like things he has suffered to attain. However, when that "thing" is a career, occupying at least half of his waking hours, it is easy to overextend his self-perception, ultimately believing that he *is* what he has done to succeed.

Most people derive an enormous sense of pride by defining themselves at least partially in terms of their accomplishments. Being "Director of X" or "Chairperson of Y" is the type of self-attribution and self-disclosure that people enjoy making. There are times, however, when feeling "you are what you do" causes extensive psychological damage, as in those cases when you are confined, restricted, or otherwise socially isolated by being seen as "what you do."

The most common problem caused by defining yourself in terms of your vocation derives from implicit personality theories. Like other attributional principles, this phenomenon applies as much to self-perception as it does to judgments made by others. Simply stated, the person who is successful in one realm—business, medicine, law— who defines himself in terms of his career will experience inordinate conflict if he is not comparably successful in all other domains. In essence, being a successful butcher, baker, or candlestick maker imposes a restriction on a person's freedom to perform related activities at less-than-superior levels.

The most problematic aspect of this circumstance— which is similar to problems brought on by encore expectations—is that self-imposed performance demands are not limited to areas of known success. Whereas a successful individual could diversify his business pursuits or take up a new hobby as a means of developing a rewarding sideline, his own burdensome expectations can force him to keep on doing only what he does best. Such a victim of The Success Syndrome thus confines his behavior only to "safe" activities for fear of risking his reputation and self-esteem in "uncharted waters."

This behavioral constraint has the secondary effect of eliminating a vast number of potentially rewarding social interactions. If a successful person initially fails to venture beyond the realm that brought him success because he fears failure, the avoidant behavior born of that anxiety will soon lead to more generalized attributions of avoidance. Specifically, as is the case with many phobic reactions, what begins as a simple fear of one element within a situation (e.g., giving a farewell speech at the office Christmas party), can generalize to a fear of the entire situation and all elements within it—skipping the party altogether and assuming that your colleagues could care less about you. The successful person who avoids new experiences because of a fear of being less than perfect can easily develop attributions that can lead to a phobia of engaging in any social interactions at all.

There is an incredibly simple, yet psychologically sophisticated, approach to treating the distress caused by being constrained to the one role identified with prior successes. Not surprisingly, it is also one of the "keys to happiness" that successful people cite most frequently when describing how they have managed to avoid the down side of success. Quite simply, this "therapeutic intervention" involves shifting the successful patient's focus from himself and his goal-seeking activities to group-oriented goals or projects. The simple act of diverting one's attention away from the self has the immediate effect of reducing stress. Performance demands and expectations get shifted from one set of overburdened shoulders to at least two sets and probably many more. In addition, and quite significantly, responsibility for potential failures gets diffused within the group as well.

Critics of this technique and its consequences would argue that with a distribution of responsibility for potential failure goes a loss of credit for potential success. This is true, and also one of the reasons why it is a strategy uniquely suited for the needs of those suffering the pressures of The Success Syndrome: they do not need any more sources of success in their lives. Those successful people who are constrained by their success, suffering the effects of social isolation, need interpersonal contacts and opportunities to free themselves from the need to sustain their image of being a "success."

Psychologists have long been aware of the manner in which group membership frees an individual from responsibilities that he would otherwise feel if alone.[14] In certain instances, the loss of individual responsibility that can result from losing one's identity within a group can lead to a variety of antisocial acts. The actions of lynch mobs and various organized hate groups are seen as being at least partially a function of this "deindividuation" that occurs when personal identities are lost within groups or beneath uniforms.[15]

Fortunately, the negative consequences of deindividuation are the exception, not the rule. The more typical response, at least within groups advocating positive philosophies, is a sense of being part of a community that has a commitment to rewarding goals shared by individuals who could not attain them on their own. Most charitable and service-oriented groups reflect these positive effects of subordinating one's personal needs to broader humanitarian concerns.

Those successful people I have interviewed who show no signs of suffering from The Success Syndrome invariably report some significant level of involvement in the work of charitable organizations. Moreover, they report deriving an enhanced sense of accomplishment from pitching in and working for goals totally unrelated to their immediate personal gain. While it is undeniable that many successful people participating in community service recognize its long-term rewards, they would be wrong to assume that testimonials were its greatest benefit. The ability to "lose themselves" and the opportunity to be a member of a worthwhile project provide more psychological rewards than all the plaques and kudos they could ever mount in their dens.

In therapy groups focused on what I call "healthy deindividuation," successful patients learn techniques that facilitate their entry into, and participation within, struc-

tured service organizations. In addition, the potential pitfalls and anxieties inherent in joining groups are addressed. Since victims of The Success Syndrome typically
develop rigid patterns of self-reliance and inflexibility that
interfere with group activities, a primary focus of all therapeutic programs at the Executive Stress Clinic is to provide patients with new behavioral skills that enable them
to join, cooperate, and follow, in contrast to their more
familiar skills of organizing, delegating, and leading.

    The psychotherapeutic programs offered at my Ex-
ecutive Stress Clinic focus primarily on helping successful
individuals restructure their distorted perceptions and debilitating attributions derived from success. These interventions form the cornerstones of programs designed to
combat disorders such as self-handicapping alcohol abuse,
success depression, and severe social isolation. Basic changes
in both self-perceptions and external expectations are needed
to permit patients victimized by success to correct the idiosyncratic views causing their distress.
    In essence, the programs offered by the Executive Stress
Clinic can enable successful people to accept the far-reaching implications of St. Luke's maxim, "To whom much is
given, much is required." More fundamental, a clinic of
this sort provides them with the capacity to separate "the
*successful* person" they are from "the *person*" they are. By
learning new ways in which to view themselves and others
who view them solely in terms of what they have done,
successful people can permanently avoid the negative consequences of The Success Syndrome.

## Chapter Thirteen

# "SUCCESS SYNDROMES" ON THE CORPORATE LEVEL

*Nothing succeeds like success.*

Alexandre Dumas


*Money changes everything.*

Cyndi Lauper

If there is one maxim universally accepted by the business community, it is Dumas's. "Them that's got shall get," goes a lyric to the Blues classic, "God bless the Child," and it appears as though Americans have bought this message hook, line, and sinker. Madison Avenue is imbued with the notion that people want to identify with, and will purchase goods and services from, those who have made it. The rest of us, it is assumed, strive to look, act, and be like people who have achieved prominence in the hope that we will somehow capture the magic and begin a string of our own successes.

The assumption that one success will be predictive of a succession of future successes is amply supported by the psychological literature. There are certain "laws" of interpersonal perception that almost force us to believe that once a person or enterprise is successful, he or it will remain so. "Successful" is what psychologists call a dispositional attribution.[1] When an individual or business enterprise achieves success, it is assumed to be a function of some sort of "internal" attribute like a natural talent or a well-developed skill, not happenstance or luck. Just as a person judged to be "hot-tempered" will be expected to yell at loved ones as well as strangers—his short fuse being dispositional, not situational—those who are successful will be expected to achieve success in all contexts. Moreover, following Dumas, once you succeed, the easier it *should be* to sustain that success or achieve new goals.

Like so many of the "laws" developed to explain human behavior, Dumas's maxim on the regenerative effects of success is frequently inaccurate. For both individuals and organizations alike, the message in the lyric from Cyndi Lauper's 1985 hit, "Money changes everything," seems sadly true. The end product of a climb to the top is often a precipitous fall to the bottom because the fruits of success—money, prestige, power, and freedom—can warp personal values and deprive individuals and enterprises of the "spiritual" impetus that got them to the top.

From a psychologist's perspective, complacency, arrogance, and a severely distorted sense of omnipotence are the destructive attitudinal changes that too often accompany financial success. Once these attitudes are manifested in an individual's interactions with others, Dumas's law is not only no longer valid, it is typically reversed. Almost immediately after money warps an achiever's attitudes, a devastating "down" side of The Success Syndrome is imminent. In short, distorted attitudes caused by financial success typically lead to failure.

Long before I began treating individuals suffering from their experience of The Success Syndrome, Texas multimillionaire Daniel R. Scoggin was describing the adverse effects of lucrative successes upon subsequent business activities. This brilliant businessman, who is the president and CEO of the T.G.I. Friday's restaurant chain, combined his business acumen and a great deal of psychological insight into the formulation of his own version of the "success syndrome." Although the "Scoggin success syndrome" details only one of the many deleterious effects derived from success, it does pinpoint a syndrome crucial to the ongoing success of commercial enterprises. Specifically, it details the way in which money can change everything about the attitudes of people who work in service-oriented industries—for the worse!

Despite his disagreement with the notion that "nothing succeeds like success," Scoggin is a living example of Dumas's maxim. Scoggin began his career as a salesman for Boise Cascade, an Idaho-based lumber and corrugated container company, and rose to the rank of eastern regional manager. He now presides over more than 100 company-owned restaurants in 31 states with average annual sales per unit ranked first in the United States in its class. In only 13 years at the helm of T.G.I. Friday's, Scoggin has created the No. 1 casual-theme restaurant chain in the United States, with gross revenues in excess of $350 million and a goal of passing the $1 billion mark before the end of this decade.

Achievements such as these have made Scoggin the focus of feature stories in periodicals such as *Forbes*, *Restaurant Business*, and *The Dallas Morning News*. Wherever and whenever he is asked about the secrets of his success, he asserts that although T.G.I. Friday's is no longer affected by the Scoggin success syndrome, it is *not* immune to the disorder. His recognizing this vulnerability and adopting a proactive approach to minimize the negative effects of financial success upon his (10,000+) employees' attitudes may underlie the obvious success and recognition he has received. As Scoggin noted repeatedly as we spoke about success: "Inherent in the success of every restaurant are the seeds of failure. These seeds are elements of the 'success syndrome.' It has happened in every single store we have opened, and in order to sustain success you must predict its occurrence and plan to do something about it."

To fully understand the Scoggin success syndrome, it is instructive to hear his description of how trying to understand reversals in the revenues of his original restaurants led to his discovery of the seeds of failure inherent in success:

In 1972 our T.G.I. Friday's in Dallas, Houston, and Atlanta were the highest grossing restaurant/bar combinations in the U.S. And in any given town we went into, we were the "in" place, the hottest thing going, written up in *Time, Newsweek, Playboy,* all the major publications. In 1973–1974, these restaurants started coming apart. The Dallas store went from $60,000 per week to $30,000. Same for Houston, and the landlords who operated on a percentage [of the gross for rent] basis were calling in and asking, "What's the deal?; our other restaurants in the area aren't having the same problems," so I knew that it wasn't an economic, competition, or weather-related problem.

When I went through the traditional process of trying to figure out what the problem was, almost everyone gave me pat answers: "That is what you get in the restaurant business . . . hit a stride and level off until your lease runs out"; "A successful restaurant hauls a pack of competitors in its wake, and we're just feeling the effects of competition." I didn't buy any of these answers and started to visit every successful bar/restaurant combination in the United States to determine what accounted for their being on their way to success, enjoying success, or on their way back down to failure.

Looking for a common ingredient to explain this pattern I found it in the seventh place I visited; a place . . . in Minneapolis. It was an "in" place, written up all over. Well, I tried to walk inside and was blocked by an arrogant doorman who made it very clear to me that he was a very powerful person, successful, at a successful place. . . . When I was finally lucky enough to be let inside, there was a bartender in what I have grown to term "the bartender's slump." You know, they can throw every bone in their body out of gear and slouch on the bar with that limp-lizard look in their eye and stare across the bar at an engaging young lady saying, "You know, darling, I am a bartender at *the* bar in town." Just to let me know that he wasn't ignorant of the fact that I was there, he passed me a glance which said that I was lucky to be there and had better be patient, and if my tip made any noise when it hit the bar, that would be the last drink I got that evening.

After I finally got my drink, it suddenly dawned on me that these people were highly successful and what's more, they were turning off everyone that they were coming in contact with! This was a common thread that I had seen in every successful restaurant or bar operation that I had visited.

According to Scoggin, what he saw at that bar, and every other successful restaurant/bar combination on the way down, were the full-blown symptoms of the Scoggin success syndrome. This disorder infects restaurants (and other successful enterprises) after opening-day anxieties have subsided. As Scoggin tells it, no business or businessman would ever suffer the Scoggin success syndrome if the attitudes and apprehensions existing immediately prior to embarking on a new business venture were maintained: "What will I do if customers don't show up?" "I'm in debt up to my ears; I'll do anything to please the customers." And so on.

As Scoggin noted in his travels and within his own T.G.I. Friday's system, the fear of failure, desire to please customers, and gratitude for initial successes when they do occur are typically not sustained once success is achieved.

He described the transformations he observed in successful restaurants in the following way:

> When a brand-new operation opens up, the employees are typically behind on their rent, car payments, something. They follow the lead of management, who'll typically be as nice and as humble as can be for the first three months. This aura of courteousness pervades a new operation. Once they become successful, everyone gets caught up on their debts, and the standard set by the boss is being ignored because they're not scared anymore. The boss is now slouching around, his tie off, shirt unbuttoned down to his navel exposing five pounds of gold hanging around his neck, saying "Touch me if you can . . . I happen to own this place." It's a daylight to darkness transformation I've seen everywhere I've been. This syndrome occurs in every restaurant we've ever opened.

A widely accepted although undocumented "truth" within the mental health professions is that most theories of human behavior are formulated by individuals experiencing or suffering from the phenomenon they observe in others. As Martin Luther noted, "It makes a difference whose ox is gored," and this rule of empathy is as applicable to developing laws of psychology as it is to the commercial modes of human interaction. In Scoggin's case, we observe a phenomenally successful businessman who steadfastly believes that one can sustain success only by maintaining attitudes that exist when an entrepreneur is uncertain of his future and fearful of failure. Since this belief is the cornerstone of the Scoggin success syndrome, I wondered about the influence exerted by a fear of failure in the formative years of his life. Putting on my "clinician's hat," I asked him about his upbringing:

I came from an extremely poor background and had a terrible fear of remaining poor. I remember going to school in San Francisco and eating in a cafeteria on Market Street and seeing these old people who were just barely able to keep life and limb together. They were alone, very, very poor, and I had a horrible fear of being like them. I was acutely aware of being one of the have-nots, knowing about the haves, and wanting to have more for myself. I think in my early business career what motivated me was that fear.

## THE "OIL WELL SYNDROME": VULNERABILITY TO THE SCOGGIN SUCCESS SYNDROME

Based upon the preceding remarks, we can clearly see that Scoggin did make use of his fear of failure (poverty) when formulating his success syndrome. But this is only part of the story. The Scoggin success syndrome maintains that money changes attitudes for the worse, converting formerly courteous and caring employees into arrogant, self-centered narcissists whose behavior drives customers away. Why, then, was Scoggin not transformed by his formidable success?

To begin with, much of Scoggin's current prosperity was born of adversity; his climb to the top was not without certain bumps and bruises, and his early successes with T.G.I. Friday's were contingent upon arduous labor. Recall that the Scoggin success syndrome was formulated *after* he noticed how, in 1973–1974, his very successful restaurants were "coming apart" as a result of employees manifesting arrogant, offensive attitudes. Yet more important than his insights derived from transient economic distress, is Scoggin's ability to create challenges in his life (the source of *eustress*), without imposing burdensome expectations on himself.

When I asked Dan Scoggin why he was *not* affected adversely by success, he said that when he did come to have money, his original fears of poverty were quickly transformed into fears of being merely ordinary. Once financial security was his, Scoggin wanted to meet challenges and succeed at previously insurmountable tasks:

> Some people work to live, some people live to achieve, and I think that's how it is in my case. Some achievers set goals that are attainable; I do that, but I always have goals that are beyond that. The one time I didn't set new goals after meeting one, I was in deep trouble. I was depressed, and I was lost, and I took a year away from work and did dumb things. But in the process I reset my goals to go beyond keeping score of what I could buy, and established a set of *internal challenges* to give value and authentic private enjoyment to my life.

As discussed earlier, once a particular goal is attained and success is in hand, the only way to maintain a positive self-image is to raise your standards or, as psychologists would say, your level of aspiration. Following the advice of Browning ("A man's reach should exceed his grasp, or what's a heaven for?"), Scoggin avoided succumbing to the success syndrome he identified by reaching for heaven. In the motivational seminars that he prepares and delivers to T.G.I. Friday's employees, Scoggin strives to instill a similar attitude in his audiences. The notion of striving to exceed one's grasp is put forth as a crucial standard for all employees to adopt if they are to avoid the failure inherent in the Scoggin success syndrome.

Yet Scoggin is a pragmatist, and a proactive one at

that. He's of the opinion that an ounce of prevention is worth a pound of cure, at least insofar as the Scoggin success syndrome is concerned. From his perspective, it makes much better sense for the financial well-being of T.G.I. Friday's to select employees with preexisting attitudes that would make them resistant to the Scoggin success syndrome, than to try to train employees who are prone by disposition to arrogance and complacency. The type of employee that Scoggin feels is particularly susceptible to the Scoggin success syndrome is one already suffering from what he calls the "oil well syndrome":

> The individuals least likely to be successful with us are the kind of people who want success because it is going to place them at the material level of existence they have always envied. They want the car, the house, the material things, but are unwilling, or haven't thought through what it takes to maintain that level of success. What they really want is to go out and drill an oil well, strike it rich, and just have that thing pumping money so they never have to do anything again. They don't want to set goals; they're the kind of people that you [S.B.] told me about, the ones with a depreciated sense of self-worth following monetary success. I've seen people come into the system with all the capabilities, intelligence, and drive to succeed, but with none of the staying power; they quit at the point of success instead of getting enjoyment out of continuing to build and sustain what they've built.

## SELECTING "SUCCESS-RESISTANT" EXECUTIVES

With his two syndromes—success and oil well—Scoggin has done much more than illustrate the power that success and money have to corrupt those who attain them.

This highly perceptive businessman has identified a major problem confronting the entire business community: how to select, reward, and promote employees who will not succumb to the effects of financial security that are capable of undermining the attitudes and work ethic that originally brought success to their business.

We can now see that the term "success-resistant," as employed in the title of this section, although at first glance humorous or possibly absurd, describes a highly desirable attribute sought by knowledgeable corporate presidents and CEOs. Anyone familiar with The Success Syndrome is aware that while success is *embraced* by all, it is poorly tolerated by many of those who achieve it. The attribute that makes "success-resistant" individuals extremely desirable is their capacity to tolerate those aspects of success—access to "oil wells," life in the fast lane—that precipitate disasterous endings like those described by the Scoggin success syndrome.

Mental health professionals are, in actuality, at a loss to identify success-resistant individuals. Industrial psychologists would *like* to develop a reliable "profile" of the person most likely to climb the ladder of success without slipping or gasping for breath before reaching the top, but as yet have been unable to do so. This is due in part to the limitless number of variables that can derail people on the fast track, and in part to a lack of sophistication in the "art" of identifying what aspects of a person's psychological makeup will malfunction under the stress of success.

The best method of identifying employees likely to manifest an oil well syndrome, or the attitude of arrogance and entitlement observed in the Scoggin success syndrome, is to rely on the judgments of successful corporate executives. As their careers prosper over time, CEOs like

Scoggin appear to develop a finely tuned set of "sensors" that seem capable of distinguishing the success-resistant employee from the others. While it is difficult to identify precisely how these "sensors" operate, the end product of their work is very apparent: the selection of employees who continually *increase* their level of aspiration and commitment to their business even after having received financial and material rewards.

The process of screening potential employees to identify those who are *not* success-resistant (i.e., prone to the Scoggin success syndrome), begins when they are "hungry" for work, or at least new and potentially rewarding work. In a sense, the person doing the screening is in a position comparable to that of confronting hungry men in need of fish or fishing lessons. With this perspective in mind, the process for identifying the success-resistant individual is fairly straightforward. Applicants susceptible to the oil well syndrome would want to be given big fish immediately and for as long as they are available. On the other hand, the success-resistant would prefer a rod, reel, hooks, and instructions in how to use them.

## HOW REWARDS TAKE THE FUN AND JOY OUT OF WORK

The Scoggin success syndrome is an elegant illustration of how success changes an individual's attitudes for the worse. Scoggin's philosophies on management include the premise that "at the center of the success syndrome you will find employees taking their success for granted and developing big-shot attitudes, while forgetting to provide the services that brought customers in [to the restaurant]." As noted above, the insight that spawned the Scoggin success syndrome was that material wealth often breeds attitudes of complacency and arrogance because it eliminates fears of failure.

There is no questioning the fact that the Scoggin success syndrome describes one of the attitudinal changes brought about by the acquisition of money. Complacency and a "screw you!" attitude toward the customer are frequently a consequence of success; support for this contention can be found wherever the subject of money is discussed. For example, success has often been accused, somewhat inappropriately, of vulgarizing whatever it touches.[2] This accusation gains credibility, however, when success is defined solely in terms of material rewards, as in money. The most famous source of support for the contention that material wealth exerts a negative influence over those who gain it is provided by the eminent psychologist/philosopher William James:

> The moral flabbiness born of the exclusive worship of the bitch-goddess SUCCESS. That—with the squalid cash interpretation put on the word success—is our national disease.[3]

James's sentiment, which is akin to the maxim of Cyndi Lauper (and others)—money changes everything—underscores the notion that money changes the person who earns it, rendering him or her too morally weak to work.

Yet many of the changes observed in those suffering pressures derived from The Success Syndrome (in its broadest definition) are not a function of success "spoiling" or pampering formerly diligent workers. More often, people become embittered and unproductive as a result of the *way* in which they are rewarded for doing something that they once enjoyed. In lay terms, successful people often stop "putting out" because the particular fruit of their labors "puts them *off*."

To understand why material rewards, particularly money, can "turn off" a once successful person, it is instructive to first consider how work differs from play. For most of us, this difference becomes apparent after comparing the amount of fun inherent in one activity over the other. In other words, a commonsense distinction between work and play involves the recognition that play is fun; an end in itself, something we *want* to do. Work, on the other hand, is a means to an end, an activity that would not necessarily engage a person's interest or energy were it not for the outcomes it produced. In the words of Mark Twain, "Work consists of whatever a body is *obliged* to do. . . . Play consists of whatever a body is not obliged to do."[4] Quite obviously, the "end" that obligates people to work is the acquisition of money.

Thus, in that pure and uncontaminated world where black is black and white is white, people are motivated to play for factors inherent in the activity itself, or what psychologists would call an *intrinsic motivation*. People are intrinsically motivated by the joys that derive from doing, not *getting*. Engaging in work, on the other hand, is motivated by factors external to the activity itself, or by what psychologists call *extrinsic motivation*.[5] Money is the most obvious extrinsic motivation for engaging in an activity not intrinsically motivating. It is the ultimate ulterior motive; a great reason for doing what we don't want, but are obliged to do.

Sadly, the pure and uncontaminated world exists only in the minds of little children, dreamers, and the insane; most things in life are not 100% black or white. It is often the case that our play is initiated to fulfill obligations (golfing with business associates to close a deal; attending parties hosted by the "right" social contacts as a means of improving business relations), while many of us have careers that are intrinsically motivating despite some aspects that border on drudgery. What this means in practical terms is that our involvement in either work or play can be expected to fall under the control of both *extrinsic* motivators (e.g., money) and *intrinsic* motivators, depending upon a variety of circumstances.

Not many problems arise from the fact that it takes extrinsic motivators such as money to engage the services of people to do work that they or others do not find appealing. Were it not for money, who would work in our nation's sanitation systems? Problems do arise, however, when huge sums of money are paid to people who work at activities that provide them with intrinsic rewards. This situation, essentially providing *two* types of reward for one activity, can make what was once play eventually seem like work.

In those instances where material rewards are great—so great that they appear capable of coercing a person to do something that he would otherwise avoid—the rewarded person typically comes to assume that "he's only in it for the money." Psychologists who have studied the negative effects of rewarding intrinsically motivated behaviors with extrinsic rewards such as money call this phenomenon an "overjustification effect."[6]

Overjustification effects derive from extrinsic rewards seeming excessive or "overjustifying" for intrinsically motivated behaviors. Paying a person to collect trash will never result in an overjustification effect unless the salary for this work is in excess of $100,000. Overjustification effects would occur, however, were someone to derive a salary of even $20,000 for watching their favorite sporting event not as a reporter, scout, coach, or interested professional, but merely as a fan.

Paying a fan to watch his favorite team play would undoubtedly evoke reactions such as: "What's the catch?" or "Why are you giving me this money—is something wrong, is there something dangerous going on?" People know that there is no such thing as a "free lunch" and "You don't get something for nothing," so when something (money) is given, there must be a reason why. The reason "why" a person is paid to do something must always include a recognition—on the part of the person or others—that the "something" in question involves a special skill or that it is aversive; it thereby requires the presence and persuasive powers of money to reward expertise or overcome resistance.

Another factor contributing to overjustification effects is that material rewards are more conspicuous to one's attention and stand out more in one's awareness than intrinsic rewards. Because of their salience, extrinsic rewards can divert a person's attention from intrinsic factors, which otherwise might have been seen as motivating his behavior. Once this sort of perceptual shift takes place—from seeing yourself as doing something because you like it, to doing something because of what it can get you—a sense of being mercenary or of prostituting yourself can develop. Should the acquisition of material rewards become so out of proportion to the task at hand that you perceive yourself as dependent upon, or a slave to, those rewards, the result is always a *decreased* involvement with the activity that elicited those feelings.

Overjustification effects are usually, but not always, observed when the role of money seems to be the dominant cause of a person's behavior. They are known to occur when the rewards provided for a given behavior seem inappropriate to the task. For example, there are several studies in the psychological literature demonstrating that children given prizes for playing games they were already involved in prior to receiving those rewards enjoyed the games less than matched counterparts who received no prizes.[7] Even verbal rewards such as praise can, under certain circumstances, evoke overjustification effects. Experimental subjects who were recipients of hearty praise following completion of an intrinsically interesting puzzle-solving game showed less desire to play with it in the future than subjects who were not praised.[8]

Venturing beyond the walls of psychological laboratories, we can easily find evidence of the aversive consequences of overjustification effects. Virtually all corporate presidents and CEOs running large organizations must be aware of the manner in which overjustification effects can have a negative impact upon job performance. It is crucial that managers determine how to regulate the flow of both their accolades and their cash bonuses lest these disrupt the motivation of their employees. In some organizations, psychologically minded CEOs have gone so far as to institute hard and fast guidelines to regulate the size and timing of bonuses. These procedures are typically instituted as a means of eliminating the disruptive consequences that would ensue if an employee assumed that his bonus implied an excessive amount of appreciation on the part of management.

In the world of professional sports, where those on salary do exactly what amateurs do for free, overjustification effects are particularly evident. Bob Lobel articulated the dilemma of most men who were "jocks" in their youth and then got paid for their involvement in athletics when older. As a youth, the intrinsic satisfaction derived from being a "jock" was sufficient to sustain his involvement in sports. However, as an adult, when he used his sports savvy to derive a millionaire's status, Bob experienced a transient disenchantment with professional sports. He became indifferent to various aspects of his sportscaster's craft due to what he termed a shift from "a producer mode to a consumer mode." In essence, sports ceased to be something to engage in for the fun of it once it became a means to the end of big money. All of the professional athletes I've treated for the stress of success report a similar phenomenon: "It was fun to play [my sport] as a kid in the [sandlot, schoolyard, gym], but now it's work. I've got to score points to justify my [bonus, salary]." This feeling helped drive Derek Sanderson to alcoholism, and has ruined a number of promising careers. Many athletes drawing huge salaries suffer the consequences of poorer attitudes, lowered motivation, and decreased performance at some point in their lucrative careers.

Jimmy Cefalo, the sportscaster for NBC's *Sunrise*, has commented that professional sports teams rarely repeat championships in back-to-back seasons.[9] In his opinion, following a successful season and the rewards it brings—in the form of bonuses, product endorsements, and the like—athletes become more concerned with filming their next commercial than with watching the films of last week's game or next week's opponent. According to Cefalo, an athlete's performance suffers when he is even slightly distracted from his work by external concerns such as savoring the fruits of last year's championship. From a psychologist's perspective, a person's performance at any intrinsically motivating task will suffer when salient rewards become the focus, as opposed to a pleasant consequence, of previously gratifying behavior.

## THE SOPHOMORE JINX

One of the more perplexing problems facing any organization that has a need to develop the skills and responsibilities of young and talented individuals is a phenomenon called the "sophomore jinx." In essence, this phenomenon describes the plight of supersuccessful, freshman employees who "bomb" in their second year on the job.

Many of these jinxed sophomores fail owing to attitudinal problems described by the Scoggin success syndrome, while others merely succumb to other stresses of success. Yet the majority of them fall victim to some form of overjustification effect. Since cash is the most widely used incentive and reward for desired behavior in business organizations, it is no wonder that young, highly motivated employees soon become jaded "organizational clones."

The sophomore jinx could easily be reduced in most organizations by supplementing cash rewards with rewards designed to enhance internal satisfaction from the job. For example, any individual who works for an organization in a capacity that involves the development of ideas (e.g., scientists of any stripe, people who write for a living, organizational VP's for development) needs freedom from mundane chores to do his work well. A valued bonus to such an individual would be "free time," devoid of organizational responsibility, to think and work without encumbrance. A reduced workload (to provide "creative time"), plus some cash bonus, would be far more rewarding to most "creative types" than cash alone.

Likewise, middle managers are typically caught between their bosses, who dictate company policy, and their supervisees, who must effect policy. Granting these middle managers more control over determining the policies they are called upon to enact would entrench a sense of involvement with their corporation's overall development, thereby ensuring a sense of intrinsic satisfaction from the job.

Incentives such as these, which reinforce an employee's intrinsic motivations, are not pie-in-the-sky fantasies for averting sophomore jinxes. Comparable incentive programs exist in many U.S. corporations that have an awareness of motivational psychology.

Dan Scoggin has instituted a reward system in his T.G.I. Friday's chain that seems ideally suited to the idiosyncratic needs of the younger employees typically hired by restaurant chains. This reward mechanism, called the "Passport System," allows employees of T.G.I. Friday's who have demonstrated skills, diligence, and intellectual competence a chance to work briefly in any one of the company's franchises across the nation and move to another company restaurant whenever they wish. In this manner, talented young employees can earn their way around the nation and return to steady employment at their T.G.I. Friday's "of origin," with 100% freedom of movement *and* the full commitment of the corporation behind their youthful wanderlust.

Scoggin's Passport System and incentive programs like it are surefire means for averting overjustification effects. By being provided with high-level rewards that do not undermine his intrinsic motivation, the talented individual finds that he retains his enthusiasm for work and becomes even more motivated to achieve new heights. Creative CEOs can design incentive systems that provide salaries and intrinsic satisfaction—the type of reward that an employee truly wants and/or needs.

When we see victims of overjustification effects lose interest in their careers after a huge success and merely "go through the motions" of their jobs, the importance of the proper incentives and reward systems becomes painfully apparent. Every organization wants to foster the development of talented "freshmen," but money does change everything, and occasionally it undermines the promise of people and things it touches. While there are really few substitutes for *appropriately earned* financial rewards, excessive financial gain can quickly turn into filthy lucre and precipitate a range of disruptive effects. Organizations supplementing appropriate financial rewards with proper psychological incentives can avert the down side of The Success Syndrome.

# EPILOGUE

*Be nice to people on your way up because you'll meet 'em on your way down.*

Jimmy Durante

I do not share the fatalism expressed by Jimmy Durante, although his comment does have some merit. A major focus of this book has been to demonstrate that success has a variety of consequences, including a great many that *will* precipitate inordinate stress and *may* herald a "fall." However, another focus of this book has been to demonstrate that everyone need not succumb to the adverse consequences of The Success Syndrome, and that the suffering of those who do can be ameliorated.

Durante's bromide would have been more useful had he elaborated on it further. Were this the case, he would have clarified why it is important for those on their way to the top to be nice to people. He would have explained that social support and friendship are two of the most effective means of combating the stress of social isolation born of success.

Alternatively, Durante might have noted that those executives who have a positive sense of self-esteem run organizations *with* confidence and *by* their inspiring example—not by rule of force, intimidation, or otherwise. These individuals developed their positive attitudes and confidence over time as a result of their *demonstrated* abilities, which were reinforced by the *approval* of others. Since it is likely—given their history of social approval—that these confident executives demonstrated the ability to get along with others, they would *not* be expected to suffer the trip "down" following success after all.

But not every successful individual has the confidence or the interpersonal skills to naturally avoid The Success Syndrome. Thus, the intent of this book in setting forth the complex set of psychological principles that account for The Success Syndrome is to forewarn and forearm the reader for the multiple consequences of success. The stress derived from success is inevitable and can be expected to touch virtually every corner of an individual's life. Yet understanding The Success Syndrome and anticipating its adverse effects makes these negative consequences more controllable and thus less stressful.

The burdensome expectations, jealousies, losses, and difficulties forming intimate personal relationships which follow in the wake of success  cannot be totally avoided but they can be planned for and mastered. For those in the throes of the down side of The Success Syndrome, the earlier discussion of my Executive Stress Clinic may provide some guidelines for addressing the stress of success. Common sense, strengthening friendships, and diversifying one's interests and activities will go a long way toward providing the balance of what is needed to ensure that The Success Syndrome will not be devastating.

The pursuit of success and its attainment are two of the most significant experiences an individual can know. Nothing, except for love, can exceed the pleasure and self-satisfaction that derive from success. As noted in the quotation by Moss Hart that opened this book, success *can* make one feel more alive, handsomer, uncommonly gifted, and indomitably secure. My aim has been to explain the syndrome that can rob success of its capacity to "change the human mechanism" so favorably—as Hart asserted— so that the desired outcomes made possible by success can be realized by all who succeed.

# REFERENCES

# INTRODUCTION

1. *U.S. News & World Report*, October 3, 1983.
2. Williams, T., "The Catastrophe of Success," *Harpers Bazaar*, January 1984, pp. 132–133.
3. Kleinfield, N. R. "What It Takes: The Life of a CEO," *The New York Times Magazine*, December 1, 1985, p. 33.
4. "The Footprints of Apollo 11," *Newsweek*, July 2, 1979, p. 19.
5. Greiff, B. S., and Munter, P. K., *Trade Offs: Executive, Family and Organizational Life* (New York: New American Library, 1980).
6. Boyd, D. P., and Gumpert, D. E., "Executives and Stress: Coping with Entrepreneurial Success," *Harvard Business Review*, March/April 1983, pp. 44–63.
7. Vare, R., "Avoiding Success," *The New York Times Magazine*, November 14, 1982, p. 40.
8. Franklin, B., *Autobiography and Other Writings*, R. B. Nye, Ed. (Boston: Houghton Mifflin, 1958).

# CHAPTER ONE

1. Lasch, C., *The Culture of Narcissism: American Life in An Age of Diminishing Expectations* (New York: Warner Books, 1979).
2. *U.S. News & World Report*, October 3, 1983, p. 60.
3. Brandt, A., "How to Think About The Rich," *Esquire*, September 1983, p. 21.

4. Berglas, S., "The Self-Handicapping Model of Alcohol Abuse," *Psychological Theories of Drinking and Alcoholism*, H. T. Blane and K. E. Leonard, Eds. (New York: Guilford Press, in press).
5. *Newsweek*, December 31, 1984, pp. 14–24.
6. Ibid., p. 17.
7. Ibid., p. 19.
8. Ibid., p. 18.
9. *U.S. News & World Report*, October 3, 1983, p. 60.
10. *U.S. News & World Report*, March 4, 1985, p. 10.
11. Ibid., p. 62.
12. *U.S. News & World Report*, October 3, 1983, p. 60.
13. Goodman, E., *At Large* (New York: Summit Books, 1981), p. 19.
14. *U.S. News & World Report*, March 4, 1985, p. 62.
15. Goldsmith, B., "The Meaning of Celebrity," *The New York Times Magazine*, December 4, 1983, p. 76.
16. Lasch, p. 47.
17. Berglas, S., "Self-Handicapping Alcohol Abuse," *Alcohol, Health and Research World*, Winter 1985/1986, *10(2)*, 46–47; 54.

## CHAPTER TWO

1. Festinger, L., "A Theory of Social Comparison Processes," *Human Relations*, 1954, pp. 117–140.
2. Huber, R. M., *The American Idea of Success* (New York: McGraw–Hill, 1971), p. 1.
3. Korda, M., *Success!* (New York: Random House, 1977), p. 237.
4. Blumenthal, M., "Ten Routes to the American Dream," *Time Magazine*, July 8, 1985, p. 58.
5. Korda, p. 237.
6. Mandell, J., "The Pillsbury Doughboy," *Esquire*, May 1985, p. 124.
7. Berglas, S., and Jones, E. E., "Drug Choice as a Self-Handicapping Strategy in Response to Noncontingent Success," *Journal of Personality and Social Psychology*, 1978, *36*, 405–417.
8. Bartlett, J., *Bartlett's Familiar Quotations*, 15th and 125th Anniversary Edition (Boston: Little, Brown, 1982), p. 637, No. 13.
9. Huber, p. 2.
10. See the definition of prestige offered by Goode, W. J., *The Celebration of Heroes: Prestige as a Social Control System* (Berkeley: University of California Press, 1978), p. 7.

11. Ross, R., and Van Den Haag, E., *The Fabric of Society*, 1957, p. 750.
12. Bendix, R., and Lipset, S. N., *Class, Status and Power*, 2nd Edition (New York: Free Press, 1966).
13. Franklin, B., *Autobiography and Other Writings*, R. B. Nye, Ed. (Boston: Houghton Mifflin, 1958), with specific quotations derived from the Introduction prepared by R. B. Nye.
14. Hollingshead, A. B., *Elmtown's Youth* (New York: Wiley, 1949), p. 450.
15. Huber, p. 7.

## CHAPTER THREE

1. Goldsmith, B. "The Meaning of Celebrity," *The New York Times Magazine*, December 4, 1983, p. 75.
2. Ibid.
3. Alpern, D. N., "Behind The Wheels," *Newsweek*, October 8, 1984, p. 50.
4. "A Spunky Tycoon Turned Superstar," *Time Magazine*, April 1, 1985, p. 35.
5. "The Wings of Frank Borman," *Newsweek*, November 12, 1984, p. 77.
6. "Iacocca: An Autobiography," *Newsweek*, October 8, 1984, p. 70.
7. For a complete description of the "mere exposure" effect, see Rubin, Z., *Liking and Loving: An Invitation to Social Psychology* (New York: Holt, Rinehart & Winston, 1973), pp. 113–134.
8. See Jones, E. E., and Gerard, H. B., *Foundations of Social Psychology* (New York: Wiley, 1967), pp. 272, 713.
9. Asch, S. E., "Forming Impressions of Personality," *Journal of Abnormal and Social Psychology*, 1946, *41*, 258–290.
10. See for example, Cronbach, L. J., "Processes Affecting Scores on 'Understanding of Others' and 'Assumed Similarity,' " *Psychological Bulletin*, 1955, *52*, 177–193.
11. "Palm Springs Dresses Down," *Newsweek*, October 29, 1984, p. 104.
12. Korda, M., *Success!* (New York: Random House, 1977), p. 54.
13. See, for example, Holmes, T. H., and Masuda, M., "Life Changes and Illness Susceptibility," *Stressful Life Events: Their Nature and Effects*, B. S. Dohrenwend and B. P. Dohrenwend, Eds. (New York: Wiley, 1974), pp. 45–72.
14. See, for example, Kanner, A. D., Coyne, J., Schaefer, C., and Lazarus, R., "Comparison of Two Modes of Stress Measurement: Daily

Hassles and Uplifts Versus Major Life Events," *Journal of Behavioral Medicine*, 1981, 4, 1–39.
15. "Occidental's One-Man Show," *Newsweek*, September 10, 1984, p. 57.
16. Ibid.
17. "Macho Men of Capitalism," *Newsweek*, October 1, 1984, p. 58.
18. "Seven Who Succeeded," *Time Magazine*, January 7, 1985, p. 42.
19. "America's Power Couple," *Newsweek*, October 31, 1983, p. 37.
20. Nelson, B., "How Does Power Affect the Powerful?" *The New York Times*, November 9, 1982, p. C3.
21. Ibid.
22. Kissinger, H. A., from *The New York Times*, January 19, 1971, quoted in Bartlett, J., *Bartlett's Familiar Quotations*, 15th and 125th Anniversary Edition (Boston: Little, Brown, 1982).

## CHAPTER FOUR

1. "Master of the Game," *Time Magazine*, January 7, 1985, p. 32.
2. Iacocca, L., *Iacocca* (New York: Bantam Books, 1984), p. 57.
3. Stockton, W., "On the Brink of Altering Life," *The New York Times Magazine*, February 17, 1980, pp. 19, 62.
4. Winerip, M., "High-Profile Prosecutor," *The New York Times Magazine*, June 9, 1985, p. 38.
5. Cotton, N. S., "Self-Esteem and Self-Esteem Regulation," *The Development and Substance of Self-Esteem in Childhood*, J. E. Mack and S. L. Ablon, Eds. (New York: International Universities Press, 1983), pp. 122–150.
6. Blanchard, K., and Johnson, S., *The One Minute Manager* (New York: Morrow, 1982).
7. Reich, C., "The Innovator," *The New York Times Magazine*, April 21, 1985, p. 30.

## CHAPTER FIVE

1. Selye, H., *The Stress of Life* (New York: McGraw–Hill, 1976).
2. Korda, M., *Success!* (New York: Random House, 1977).
3. Shaughnessy, D., "Behind the Legend," *The Boston Globe*, April 19, 1985, p. 68.

4. *Newsweek*, December 9, 1985, p. 23.
5. Ferraro, G., "Ferraro: My Story," *Newsweek*, October 7, 1985, p. 72.
6. Ibid., p. 80.
7. "Instant Riches Bring Problems for Many," *The New York Times*, June 4, 1978.
8. Kelley, H. H., *Attribution in Social Interaction* (Morristown, N.J.: General Learning Press, 1971).
9. Brehm, J. W., *A Theory of Psychological Reactance* (New York: Academic Press, 1966).
10. Festinger, L., "Wish, Expectation, and Group Standards as Factors Influencing Levels of Aspiration," *Journal of Abnormal and Social Psychology*, 1942, 184–200.
11. See Berglas, S., "I Have Some Good News and Some Bad News: You're the 'Greatest'." The Disruptive Effects of Positive Feedback. Unpublished manuscript, Department of Psychology, Duke University, 1976; and Berglas, S., Strategies of Externalization and Performance: The Facilitative Effect of Disruptive Drugs. Doctoral dissertation, Department of Psychology, Duke University, 1976.

## CHAPTER SIX

1. James, W., *The Principles of Psychology* (Chicago: Encyclopaedia Britannica, 1952), p. 200.
2. Gershwin, G., *Porgy and Bess*, "I Got Plenty O'Nuttin."
3. Collier, P., and Horowitz, D. *The Kennedys: An American Dream* (New York: Summit Books, 1984), p. 357.
4. Ibid.
5. Kelley, H. H., *Attribution in Social Interaction* (Morristown, N.J.: General Learning Press, 1971).
6. Cronbach, L. J., "Processes Affecting Scores on 'Understanding of Others' and 'Assumed Similarity,' " *Psychological Bulletin*, 1955, 52, 177–193.
7. *People Magazine*, "Adventure. Lost Love, New Films: At 29 Candy Bergen is Growing Up," July 28, 1975, p. 48.
8. Williams, T., "The Catastrophe of Success," *Harpers Bazaar*, January 1984, pp. 132–133.
9. See, for example, Berglas, S., "I Have Some Good News and Some Bad News: You're the 'Greatest'." The Disruptive Effects of Positive Feedback. Unpublished manuscript, Department of Psychology,

Duke University, 1976; and Berglas, S., Strategies of Externalization and Performance: The Facilitative Effect of Disruptive Drugs. Doctoral dissertation, Department of Psychology, Duke University, 1976.

10. See Carson, R. C., *Interaction Concepts of Personality* (Chicago: Aldine, 1969), or Foa, U. G., and Foa, E. B., *Social Structures of the Mind* (Springfield, Illinois: Thomas, 1974).

11. Jones, E. E., *Ingratiation* (New York: Appleton–Century–Crofts, 1964).

12. Steinem, G., "Patti Davis," *Ms. Magazine*, January 1986, pp. 78, 100.

13. Berglas, S., "I Have Some Good News and Some Bad News: You're the 'Greatest'." The Disruptive Effects of Positive Feedback. Unpublished manuscript, Department of Psychology, Duke University, 1976.

## CHAPTER SEVEN

1. See Radloff, R., "Social Comparison and Ability Evaluation," *Journal of Experimental Social Psychology*, 1966, Supplement 1, 6–26; and Raph, J. B., Goldberg, M. L., and Passow, A. H., *Bright Underachievers* (New York: Teachers College Press, 1966).

2. Iscoe, I., " 'I Told You So': The Logical Dilemma of the Bright Underachieving Child," *Underachievement*, M. Kornrich, Ed. (Springfield, Illinois: Thomas, 1966).

3. Ibid.

4. See House, J. S., "Occupational Stress and Coronary Heart Disease: A Review and Theoretical Integration," *Journal of Health and Social Behavior*, March 1974, *15(1)*, 12–27; and Parker, D. A., Parker, E. S., and Harford, T. C., "Status Inconsistency and Drinking Patterns Among Working Men and Women," *Alcoholism: Clinical and Experimental Research*, Vol. 2, No. 2 (April 1978).

## CHAPTER EIGHT

1. See, for example, Seligman, M. E. P., *Helplessness* (San Francisco: Freeman, 1975).

2. See, for example, Lazarus, R. S., and Launier, R., "Stress related transactions between person and environment," *Perspectives in In-*

*teractional Psychology*, L. A. Pervin and M. Lewis, Eds. (New York: Plenum Press, 1978), pp. 287–327.

3. Bandura, A., "Self Efficacy: Toward a Unifying Theory of Behavioral Change," *Psychological Review*, 1977, *84*, 191–215.

4. Berglas, S., "Self-Handicapping and Self-Handicappers: A Cognitive/Attributional Model of Interpersonal Self-Protective Behavior," *Perspectives in Personality*, Volume 1, R. Hogan and W. H. Jones, Eds. (Greenwich, Connecticut: JAI Press, 1985), pp. 235–270.

5. "The Footprints of Apollo 11," *Newsweek*, July 2, 1979, p. 19.

## CHAPTER NINE

1. Leaming, B., "Orson Welles: The Unfilled Promise," *The New York Times Magazine,* July 14, 1985, p. 18.

2. See Jones, E. E., and Berglas, S., "Control of Attributions about the Self Through Self-Handicapping Strategies: The Appeal of Alcohol and the Role of Underachievement," *Personality and Social Psychology Bulletin*, 1978, *4*, 200–206; and Berglas, S., "Self-Handicapping and Self-Handicappers: A Cognitive/Attributional Model of Interpersonal Self-protective Behavior," *Perspectives in Personality*, Volume 1, R. Hogan and W. H. Jones, Eds. (Greenwich, Connecticut: JAI Press, 1985), pp. 235–270.

3. See Berglas, S., "Toward a Typology of Self-Handicapping Alcohol Abusers," *Advances in Applied Social Psychology*, M. J. Saks and L. Saxe, Eds. (Hillsdale, N.J.: Lawrence Erlbaum, in press), 3; and Berglas, S., "The Self-Handicapping Model of Alcohol Abuse," *Psychological Theories of Drinking and Alcoholism*, H. T. Blane and V. E. Leonard, Eds. (New York: Guilford Press, in press).

4. See Berglas, S., and Jones, E. E., "Drug Choice as a Self-Handicapping Strategy in Response to Noncontingent Success," *Journal of Personality and Social Psychology*, 1978, *36*, 405–417; and Tucker, J. A., Vuchininch, R. E., and Sobell, M. B., "Alcohol Consumption as a Self-Handicapping Strategy," *Journal of Abnormal Psychology*, 1981, *90*, 220–230.

5. Berglas, S., "Self-Handicapping and Self-Handicappers: A Cognitive/Attributional Model of Interpersonal Self-Protective Behavior," *Perspectives in Personality*, Volume 1, R. Hogan and W. H. Jones, Eds. (Greenwich, Connecticut: JAI Press, 1985), pp. 235–270.

6. Ibid.

## CHAPTER TEN

1. See, for example, Fenichel, O., *The Psychoanalytic Theory of Neurosis* (New York: Norton, 1945); and Cavenar, J. O., and Werman, D. S., "Origins of the Fear of Success," *American Journal of Psychiatry*, 1981, *138*, 1.
2. Fenichel, p. 457.
3. See Freud, S., "Some Character Types Met Within Psycho-Analytic Work" (1916), *Complete Psychological Works: Standard Edition*, Volume 14, edited and translated by J. Strachey (London: Hogarth Press, 1958); and Schuster, D. B., "On Fear of Success," *Psychiatry*, 1955, *29*, 412–420, or Szekely, L., "Success, Success Neurosis and the Self," *British Journal of Medical Psychology*, 1950, *33*, 45.
4. Fenichel, p. 243.
5. See Horner, M. S., Sex Differences in Achievement Motivation and Performance in Competitive and Noncompetitive Situations. Doctoral dissertation, University of Michigan, 1968, *Dissertation Abstracts International*, 1969, *30*, 407B (University of Microfilms No. 69-12, 135); and Horner, M. S., "Toward an Understanding of Achievement-Related Conflicts in Women," *Journal of Social Issues*, 1972, *28*, 157–176.

## CHAPTER ELEVEN

1. Brenner, M., "Growing Up Kennedy," *Vanity Fair*, February 1986, p. 55.
2. Ibid., pp. 57–59.
3. See, for example, Lerner, M. J., "The Justice Motive in Social Behavior: Introduction," *Journal of Social Issues*, 1975, *31*, 1–19.
4. Meissner, W. W., "Theories of Personality and Psychopathology: Classical Psychoanalysis," *Comprehensive Textbook of Psychiatry/III*, H. I. Kaplan, A. M. Freedman, and B. J. Sadock, Eds. (Baltimore: Williams & Wilkins, 1980), pp. 631–728.
5. Barthel, J., "Julie Christie: Simply Gorgeous . . . and Awfully Smart," *Cosmopolitan*, February 1986, p. 187.
6. Chang, H K., "The Prime Test of Connie Chung," *Savvy*, February 1986, p. 29.
7. McCabe, B., "The Stress of Success," *The Boston Globe*, November 14, 1984, pp. 40, 42.

8. Ibid.
9. Ibid.
10. Kobasa, S. C., Maddi, S. R., and Kahn, S., "Hardiness and Health: A Prospective Study," *Journal of Personality and Social Psychology*, 1982, 42, 168–177.

## CHAPTER TWELVE

1. Jones, E. E., Kanouse, D. E., Kelley, H. H., Nisbett, R. E., Valins, S., and Weiner, B., *Attribution: Perceiving the Causes of Behavior* (Morristown, N.J.: General Learning Press, 1971).
2. Jones, E. E., and Davis, K. E., "From Acts to Disposition: The Attribution Process in Person Perception," *Advances in Experimental Social Psychology*, Volume 2, L. Berkowitz, Ed. (New York: Academic Press, 1965), p. 220.
3. Heider, F., *The Psychology of Interpersonal Relations* (New York: Wiley, 1958).
4. Jones and Davis, pp. 219–266.
5. Kelley, H. H., *Attribution in Social Interaction* (Morristown, N.J.: General Learning Press, 1971).
6. Festinger, L., "A Theory of Social Comparison Processes," *Human Relations*, 1954, pp. 117–140.
7. See Beck, A. T., Rush, A. J., Shaw, B. F., and Emery, G., *Cognitive Therapy of Depression* (New York: Guilford Press, 1979); and Meichenbaum, D., Ed., *Cognitive Behavior Modification: An Integrative Approach* (New York: Plenum Press, 1977).
8. Ibid.
9. Aronson, E., "The Psychology of Insufficient Justification: An Analysis of Some Conflicting Data," *Cognitive Consistency*, S. Feldman, Ed. (New York: Academic Press, 1966), pp. 115–133.
10. Heider, F., *The Psychology of Interpersonal Relations* (New York: Wiley, 1958).
11. Jones, E. E., "The Rocky Road from Acts to Dispositions," *American Psychologist*, 1979, 34, 107–117.
12. See, for example, Bem, D. J., "Self-Perception Theory," *Advances in Experimental Social Psychology*, Volume 6, L. Berkowitz, Ed. (New York: Academic Press, 1972), pp. 1–62; and Laird, J. D., and Berglas, S., "Individual Differences in the Effects of Engaging in Counterattitudinal Behavior," *Journal of Personality*, 1975, 43, 286–305.

13. Ibid.
14. Kelley, H. H., and Thibaut, J. W., "Group Problem Solving," *The Handbook of Social Psychology*, G. Lindzey and E. Aronson, Eds. (Reading, Mass.: Addison–Wesley, 1969), p. 86.
15. Zimbardo, P. G., "The Human Choice: Individuation, Reason, and Order Versus Deindividuation, Impulse, and Chaos," *Nebraska Symposium on Motivation, 1969*, W. J. Arnold and D. Levine, Eds. (Lincoln: University of Nebraska Press, 1970).

## CHAPTER THIRTEEN

1. Jones, E. E., and Davis, K. E., "From Acts to Disposition: The Attribution Process in Person Perception," *Advances in Experimental Social Psychology*, Volume 2, L. Berkowitz, Ed. (New York: Academic Press, 1965), pp. 219–266.
2. Bartlett, J., *Bartlett's Familiar Quotations*, 15th and 125th Anniversary Edition (Boston: Little, Brown, 1982), p. 670, No. 11.
3. Ibid., p. 648, No. 4.
4. Ibid., p. 622, No. 12.
5. See, for example, Deci, E. L., "Effects of Externally Mediated Rewards on Intrinsic Motivation," *Journal of Personality and Social Psychology*, 1971, *18*, 105–115; and Deci, E. L., *Intrinsic Motivation* (New York: Plenum Press, 1975).
6. See, for example, Lepper, M. R., Greene, D., and Nisbett, R. E., "Undermining Children's Interest with Extrinsic Rewards: A Test of the 'Overjustification' Hypothesis," *Journal of Personality and Social Psychology*, 1970, *16*, 291–298; and Notz, W. W., "Work Motivation and the Negative Effects of Extrinsic Rewards," *American Psychologist*, 1975, *30*, 884–891.
7. See, for example, Kruglanski, A. W., Alon, A., and Lews, T., "Retrospective Misattribution and Task Enjoyment," *Journal of Personality and Social Psychology*, 1968, *9*, 133–141; Greene, D., and Casady, M., "Intrinsic Motivation: How to Turn Play Into Work," *Psychology Today*, September 1974, *8*, 49–54; and Mantell, D. M., "The Tricky Business of Giving Rewards," *Psychology Today*, September 1974, *8*, 52.
8. Ibid.
9. Broadcast on December 9, 1985.

# INDEX